English for Business Communication

Second Edition

A short course consisting of five modules:
Cultural diversity and socialising, Telephoning,
Presentations, Meetings and Negotiations

Teacher's Book

Simon Sweeney

CAMBRIDGE
UNIVERSITY PRESS

CAMBRIDGE UNIVERSITY PRESS
Cambridge, New York, Melbourne, Madrid, Cape Town,
Singapore, São Paulo, Delhi, Mexico City

Cambridge University Press
The Edinburgh Building, Cambridge CB2 8RU, UK

www.cambridge.org
Information on this title: www.cambridge.org/9780521754507

First published 1997
Second Edition 2003
8th printing 2012

A catalogue record for this publication is available from the British Library

ISBN 978-0-521-75450-7 Teacher's Book
ISBN 978-0-521-75449-1 Student's Book
ISBN 978-0-521-75451-4 Audio Cassette Set
ISBN 978-0-521-75452-1 Audio CD Set (2 CDs)

Contents

Introduction to the Second Edition

This second edition provides improvements to the overall design and appearance of the book as well as various small changes and updating of material. The most important content change is the introduction of more practice exercises in response to users' requests. See the paragraph *Quick Communication Check* below.

Aims of the course

The course is intended as an opportunity for intermediate-level students to develop confidence and fluency in five key communication contexts: socialising, telephoning, presenting information, participating in meetings and handling negotiations. The course has twin aims: *improving communication technique* and *developing and consolidating the target language* appropriate to the above communication contexts.

A further key aim is the *development of effective learning strategies* for both language and communication skills. The teacher's role in this is critical. It is important that certain principles are upheld, such as the need for preparation of communication tasks, the importance of practice, and the need for linking the teaching objectives with perceived professional needs. The students should be encouraged to reflect on their own performance, to identify ways in which it can be improved, and to monitor both the accuracy of their language and the effectiveness of their communication skills.

The course is primarily geared towards *improving speaking and listening skills*, though reading and writing tasks are also included. Part of the method for the development of fluency and confidence in speaking is the importance of involving students in as much discussion as possible. As a skills-driven course this is especially suitable, as students are encouraged to make their own suggestions based on their own experience, however limited. There is plenty of scope for eliciting students' ideas, impressions and opinions. Classes should be geared towards as much participation as possible. Everyone has experience of all five of the skill areas treated in the course, whether in English or in their own language.

Structure

The five modules can be studied consecutively as a conventional course. However, with some students a module may be studied where specific training in one area of communication skills is required.

There is, nonetheless, a certain logic in the order of the five modules. The first module, Socialising, is a scene setter. It establishes the teaching and learning approach used in the course. The second module, Telephoning, treats a fairly restrictive amount of language as is typical in telephoning. The third, Presentations, is in many ways the core of the course, as skills involved in presenting are often a feature of participating in meetings and negotiations. However, the more interactive nature of the latter two contexts is reflected in the nature of the material in the final two modules. These two, and the Presentations module, contain many recommendations for effective communication strategies and at the same time build up the students' repertoire in terms of language.

The final module, Negotiations, is perhaps, unsurprisingly, the most challenging in terms of language. In many ways, but partly because the language is more complex, effective study of the final module is dependent on having already dealt with the previous module on Meetings.

Listening material

There are over 80 different recordings in the book. The tasks accompanying them range from initial general comprehension points to understanding important details.

The first listening typically concentrates on meaning. Students are asked to identify key information. Check carefully that these main points are understood. It is important that meaning is established before students are asked to think about language. As a general rule, teaching aims should keep these two activities separate. The distinction should be made clear to the students and should influence students' developing learning strategies.

The second listening task normally focuses on the target language for the unit in question. Encourage students to repeat what they hear and to make notes. Writing down new language normally aids recall, but not all students can be persuaded to do this. In any case, avoid slowing down lessons for excessive writing of models from the tape.

Occasional writing – and even use of dictation – can be helpful.

Some of the later listening material in the final module on Negotiations is more difficult than the earlier modules.

Pronunciation work

There is little overt treatment of pronunciation features in the course. However, it is an option to include this aspect of language training with this material. It is recommended that if you want to spend additional time to focus on features of phonology, the course does offer good, authentic-sounding dialogues. These can be used to sensitise students to the implications of stress, intonation, pausing and thought groups. For further guidance on these aspects, see *Speaking Clearly* (Cambridge University Press, 1991).

Reading texts

Throughout the book, certain principles relating to efficient reading techniques should be upheld. Explain that it is not necessary to understand every word. The objective is to understand the main ideas. Detailed reading or studying of texts is neither desirable nor is it required.

The tasks accompanying reading texts mainly relate to the identification of key points and are designed to stimulate students' thoughts and ideas on the topics included.

Language Checklists

The Language Checklist at the end of each unit is a summary of some of the key language that has been introduced in the unit or that can be used in practice tasks and role plays. The Language Checklists are not prescriptive and offer only a sample of the sort of language that can be used. They are included as a support to students, as a possible self-study resource and as quick reference material.

Always check that students understand the phrases offered and that they are able to pronounce them correctly. Remind them that they can be selective, choosing the phrases they prefer, or even alternatives not included in the Checklists.

The Checklists are useful in preparation for the role plays in each unit. Students should also refer back to previous Checklists when they need to.

Quick Communication Check

Each unit now includes a page of exercises designed to offer an additional check on students' learning. The exercises reflect the target language in each unit, typically represented in *Language Checklists*. These exercises are desinged for self-study use, having an integrated answer key on each page. The *Quick Communication Check* thus serves as further practice, as consolidation, and as a simple test to check student's learning.

Skills Checklists

The Skills Checklists summarise the key points of technique for effective communication skills as introduced in each unit. In some cases, further points are included, either for discussion in class or as additional recommendations for students to think about in their own time.

Like the Language Checklists, the Skills Checklists are intended as a source of reference for future work, especially in preparing for telephone calls, presentations, meetings or negotiations where the language used will be English.

Transfer tasks

In most cases the aim of the Transfer tasks is to have students practise target language in defined communication contexts that relate directly to their own immediate environment, their home, their studies or their work. In this way the Transfers aim to create a bridge between the classroom and the student's world.

Timing

Most units will take around three hours. Approximate recommended timings are given in the Teacher's Book for each section of each unit. Guide times include neither any material marked as optional nor the Transfer tasks. The latter require homework or out-of-class preparation.

The times suggested are approximate and will vary according to the preferences and competence of the students involved, as well as student numbers. It is important not to labour the material. The tasks are intended to be fairly quick, but use your discretion. Clearly with extended role plays or where preparation is involved there may be some variation beyond the times suggested.

1 Building a relationship

AIMS
- Cross-cultural understanding (1)
- Welcoming visitors
- Small talk: keeping the conversation going

Briefing

This module looks at issues relating to working with professionals from other countries where cultural misunderstandings may cause embarrassment. It relates closely to the later module on Meetings. This unit focuses on developing personal relationships and mutual understanding between business partners. Unit 2 looks more directly at socialising within a business context, invitations, entertaining, and eating out.

The unit begins with an ice-breaker as a chance to develop small talk, before looking specifically at working with British and American people, together with suggestions on preparing for contacts with other countries. Knowledge and understanding is essential in order to get on well with one's partners from other countries. Socialising is instrumental in this: it is about *making relations*.

The second section deals with welcoming visitors and helping them to feel at ease. This theme is used as a lead-in to small talk, which is developed in the final section of the unit and again in Unit 2. Small talk is looked at in terms of various topics and how to keep conversation going. There is a lot of scope for discussion of students' own ideas in the unit. The Transfer includes an option on a small research project. Think about the extent to which your students may travel to other countries or are likely to receive visitors. This is important. In the latter case, discuss which aspects of the students' own country, town or culture might be interesting or unusual for a visitor.

1:1 situation

Many of the activities which lend themselves to discussion and brainstorming will require more support from you. Prompt and elicit thoughts from the student and feed in your own ideas and those included here. There are two role plays where you will need to take a part, as well as two dialogues based on flow charts where you will need to take the right-hand role in eventual practice. With more competent speakers, you may be able to add variations, thus increasing the need for spontaneity on the part of the student.

Timing: 3 hours

1 Cross-cultural understanding (1)

1 Circulate the groups, prompting comment on the photograph. Different students will comment on different things, but draw out ideas on:

- where it might be (country / hotel / factory / office, etc.)
- why they are there (for a meeting / seminar / new venture / chance / tourism, etc.)
- what kind of relationships are represented (friends / new business partners / same company, etc.)
- topics of conversation (business / non-business, hobbies, interests, small talk such as weather, travel, plans, the hotel, travel, colleagues, other countries, etc.)
- what they *won't* be talking about …

For five minutes, get groups of students to act out a typical situation as shown in the photograph. Join in yourself, exaggerating your speech patterns, encouraging a playful and humorous approach to the exercise. Then discuss issues arising from the illustration:

- Humour. Ask to what extent humour enters into business relationships – or even jokes. In some countries, such as Britain, joking is often used to relieve tension. In others, such as Germany, that might be regarded as flippant or unprofessional. Sean O'Casey, the Irish playwright, said that the Irish turn a crisis into a joke and a joke into a crisis.
- Women in business. In which cultures is this unlikely? Where are women having an increasingly prominent role in business? (Italy and the UK are examples, although less than 10% of company executives in the UK are women.) In some countries, despite legislation aimed at improving career opportunities for women, few reach the top (Norway, for example, although the field of politics is an exception).
- Alcohol and business. In cultures where alcohol is taboo, this is, of course, not an issue. However, while it is not unusual to have a glass of wine or a beer with lunch in Europe, it is very bad form to drink too much. In Italy, a nation of wine drinkers, it is very unusual to drink outside meal times, whereas in Sweden it is not unusual to have a beer with colleagues after work.
- Coffee. In many countries, coffee and business seem inextricably linked. Coffee seems to be what cements relationships, everywhere from Saudi Arabia to Argentina, via North America and Norway.
- Tea. In China and Japan, tea is more popular.

2 After ten minutes' discussion of these issues to set the theme for the module, go on to the reading task. Ask students to read the text and quickly decide what is the main idea expressed in the text.

Answer: Everybody is different. Signals mean different things to people of different cultures.

3 If necessary, allow a second reading to find the answers.
   a) Eye contact is important. Not maintaining eye contact indicates someone who is unfriendly, insecure, untrustworthy, inattentive and impersonal. But it is considered rude to stare. Americans signal interest and comprehension by bobbing their heads or grunting.
   b) Similar to Americans where eye contact is concerned. The English (sic)* pay strict attention to a speaker, listen carefully, and blink their eyes to let the speaker know he / she has been heard and understood.
   c) Taught to direct their gaze at their teacher's Adam's apple or tie knot.
   d) A gesture of respect.
   e) If a person of a lower class stares at someone of a higher class.
   f) Anger.

* *Note:* It is a small but significant point that the text, from an American source, speaks of 'the English'. Many foreigners refer to 'the English' when perhaps it would be more correct to say 'the British'. Discuss with learners what the terms Britain, the UK, Northern Ireland, Wales, Scotland and England refer to. Incidentally, the British often make the same mistake when they refer to Holland, which is actually a region of the Netherlands.

4 Introduce the question by asking why some sort of research is a good idea before doing business with people from different countries or cultures.
   a) Elicit / Suggest that:
   - partnerships need to be built on trust and shared understanding
   - initial research can help one know more about potential partners and their country, so avoiding embarrassment.

Think about possibly taboo subjects, such as:
   - politics in countries where open political diversity is not tolerated, or where democracy has a meaning different to your understanding of the term
   - talking about family relationships

- alcohol and certain foods
- discussing business too early, etc.

Refer to the Skills Checklist. Fundamental things to consider include:
- some basic geographical knowledge
- some knowledge of political and economic conditions
- religion and specific customs
- public holidays
- attitudes and expectations regarding entertaining visitors
- business conventions.

▭ ⊚ b) Introduce the recording. The speaker is an experienced negotiator, used to dealing with people from varied cultural backgrounds. He suggests seven areas that are important for someone planning to do business across a cultural frontier. Ask students to identify six of them.

Key

The following seven areas are mentioned:
- the actual political and economic situation
  - stability
  - trends
  - outlook
- infrastructure
  - telecommunications
  - transport
- religion / language
- geography / history
- culture / customs
  - people
  - food / drink / socialising
- attitudes / families
- business customs / conventions.

Option

As a further discussion point to develop, it might be interesting to ask students if they think this type of research is as important when one is planning to receive a visitor as it is when one plans to go abroad. In many cases, similar research would be advisable in both instances.

Tapescript

INTERVIEWER: So if you are going on a business trip, or meeting someone from another country – perhaps a different culture – what do you need to think about?

PETER: Well, it's not so obvious. I always try to know something about the actual political and economic situation in the other country – the politics, the economics. I should always know something about that, about what's happening. Also if I'm going abroad, I find out a little about the infrastructure – I mean the telecommunications, the transportation, that sort of thing.

INTERVIEWER: And do you find out about the general background, basic information about the country?

PETER: The culture, yes. Certainly, the religion, the language – I might learn a few polite phrases – the geography, maybe a little history. And how people live, what kind of culture it is, how people socialise, food, drink, all that is very important.

INTERVIEWER: What about family life?

PETER: Yes, that too. How families live, if private life and business ever mix … and also business customs and conventions. I don't want to be surprised by anything.

End by saying the list is not closed – there are plenty of other things one could also mention.

Discussion

Facilitate a very brief discussion on the value of the points included in this section. Students may identify particularly useful considerations to think about. Refer again to the Skills Checklist.

Ask again why preparation for contact across culture is important. Points to bring out include:
- it is a question of courtesy that one should be interested in one's business partners and in their countries
- tact and consideration are important
- knowing something about your partners can save embarrassment
- one will not be expected to be an expert: most people will be tolerant, so long as goodwill and good manners are evident.

Timing: 10 minutes

2 Welcoming visitors

Welcoming visitors involves making people feel relaxed and comfortable in a new environment. An essential part of this is small talk – or making conversation which is not directly concerned with reaching a business deal. The theme of small talk is developed in more detail later in the unit.

Read the opening questions, making sure students understand the focus of this section. Elicit suggested answers:

What happens when a visitor arrives with an appointment to visit a company?
- goes to reception
- introduces himself / herself / states reason for visit (who?)
- is taken to / met by the right person.

What are the typical stages of the first meeting? Suggest the first stage to the students: welcome and introductions. What might follow? Use the board or OHP to illustrate this structure.

Stages of a meeting

Welcome and introductions
|
Small talk / Settling in
|
Preliminaries / Plan for the visit
|
Begin discussions

What conversations take place (in stage two above)?
- offer of refreshments
- questions about trip
- first visit / previous visits

- length of stay / hotel, etc.
- special interests / needs
- reference to previous contact / other small talk.

1 Introduce the recording at Evco S.A. and play once. Elicit answers:
a) The meeting is quite informal. They use first names, they interrupt each other a little and generally seem relaxed.
b) They have never met: Louise and Klaus have spoken on the phone a couple of times.
c) Klaus wants to buy some fish to take home.

2 Play the recording again. Given the situation, Louise's interruption is probably acceptable, as is the immediate use of first names. On the other hand, Lars begins to talk about the programme for the day quite quickly. Poor Klaus! This is a bit soon, surely! Let's hope they allow their visitor more time to relax with more small talk and a sit-down.

Option

Decide whether to spend more time on the language in this extract. Perhaps highlight language for: introductions / questions about the trip / taking of coat / offering refreshments / referring to programme for the day, etc. Notice too how the small talk begins in discussing the weather and the fish. Ask learners how the conversation could have developed – if Lars had not decided to get down to business.

Note: The participants in this conversation are lucky. Klaus asks about fish and the ice is broken. Sometimes getting conversation going can be difficult. Point out that the module contains ideas for dealing with problems like this, beginning with the next section in this unit.

Tapescript

KLAUS: Hello, my name's Klaus Ervald. I've an appointment …

LOUISE: Oh hello, Klaus, I'm Louise Scott. We've spoken on the phone a couple of times. Nice to meet you.

KLAUS: It's nice to be here.

LOUISE: Oh – let me take your coat.

KLAUS: Thanks.

LOUISE: Oh, here's Lars. Lars, this is Klaus, he's just arrived.

LARS: Hello, Klaus. Pleased to meet you … and welcome to Evco.

KLAUS: Thanks.

LARS: Is this your first visit to Sweden?

KLAUS: No, I've been to Stockholm two or three times but it's my first visit to Malmö.

LOUISE: Klaus, let me get you a drink.

KLAUS: Yes, I'd like a tea, if possible, thanks.

LOUISE: Sure. With milk, or lemon?

KLAUS: With lemon, please – and sugar.

LOUISE: Right.

LARS: Did you have a good trip?

KLAUS: Absolutely no problems.

LARS: That's good. You did fly, didn't you – to Gothenberg?

KLAUS: Yes, that's right, then I drove down here.

LARS: Oh that's good. Malmö can be a little wet at this time of the year … you'll have to come back in the summer.

KLAUS: Oh, I'd like that. I always like coming to Sweden – and ah! A problem! I need some fish. Can you advise me? I always take back some fish, some salmon.

LARS: Oh, yes, gravlax.

KLAUS: And pickled herring too, in tomato sauce and the other one with onions and dill and pepper. Can you suggest a good place to get some?

LOUISE: Gravlax? It's always wonderful … the airport might be the best place. And the herring, too.

KLAUS: Okay, I'll have to get to the airport early. If I'm late, I might miss the plane. I can't go home without the fish!

LARS: No! Certainly not. Well, we'll get you some for lunch anyway!

LOUISE: Okay, here's some tea.

KLAUS: Oh, you're very kind.

LARS: So, apart from fish, can I explain the programme – I think we sent you an outline for the day – if you agree, we could start with a video which explains some of our services and then we could have a look at a few reports on campaigns …

3 Explain that the focus here is on offering assistance and stating one's needs. Start by asking the students to suggest ways to:

- offer assistance
- accept or decline such offers
- state one's needs.

▭ ◉ Then introduce the situation. Play the tape once.

Key

a) to send an email
c) drink
b) to send some flowers to his ex-wife
d) newspaper
e) taxi

Tapescript

PETER: Yes, that's all right. I'm a little early – I can wait a few minutes.

STEPHANIE: Well, can I get you a drink of something – a tea or a coffee, perhaps?

PETER: No, I'm fine thanks – but there is one thing – I'd like to send an email, a file on this disk, if I may – it's rather urgent.

STEPHANIE: Yes, of course. You can use my computer.

PETER: Thanks, that would be good.

STEPHANIE: Let me show you… Here you are. You can use this.

PETER: Thank you very much.

STEPHANIE: Anything else? Do you need anything to read, the *Economist* or something, while you're waiting?

PETER: No, it's okay. I'll send this email then I can prepare some work while I'm waiting.

STEPHANIE: Right, I'll leave you for a moment.

PETER: Thanks. Oh, one other thing, I need to send some flowers to my ex-wife. Today is the fifth anniversary of our divorce. She didn't like all the travelling I did. I think some flowers from Australia would be rather appropriate, don't you?

STEPHANIE: Er, perhaps! Right, I'll get you a number for Interflora or something like that. Maybe you have a special message you'd like to send with the flowers?

PETER: Yes, I'll think of one.

STEPHANIE: And this evening, will you need a cab to your hotel?

PETER: No, it's only five minutes. I'll walk.

Language focus option

If you think it appropriate, ask students to identify the phrases in the dialogue which concern offering assistance and talking about one's needs.

Note: students are likely to know phrases like *I'd like … / Could you get me …* but are less likely to use introductory expressions like *There is one thing I need* or *I wonder if you could help me.*

Practice 1

Procedure

- Whole class perform the dialogue in pairs.
- Switch roles and repeat.
- You prompt where necessary, listening to parts from three or four pairs.
- Give group feedback, commenting on good language and problems.
- Select a couple of pairs to perform for the class.
- Finally, play the model version on the tape and discuss points arising.

Language focus option

Use the tape to focus on language of stating needs, offering assistance.

Tapescript

VISITOR: Hello, my name's Henrik van der Linden from Amtel. I have an appointment with Sandra Bates.

RECEPTIONIST: Oh, yes, Mr van der Linden. Welcome to Datalink. Ms Bates will be along in a few minutes. She's just finishing a meeting. Can I get you something to drink?

VISITOR: No thanks, I'm fine. Er, but I wonder if I could use a phone?

RECEPTIONIST: Yes, of course. And anything else … if you need to send an email or anything …

VISITOR: No, it's okay, just the phone.

RECEPTIONIST: Right, well you can use this one.

VISITOR: Thanks. Allô.

(*a few minutes later*)

VISITOR: Pas du tout… Au revoir. Thank you very much.

RECEPTIONIST: Not at all. If there's anything else you need, please ask.

VISITOR: Yes, I was wondering how far is it to the station?

RECEPTIONIST: It's about two miles – ten minutes by taxi. Shall I book one?

VISITOR: Er, yes, thank you. That would be good. Can we say four o'clock?

RECEPTIONIST: Right, I'll do that. Oh, I think Ms Bates is free now. Shall I take you to her office?

VISITOR: Thanks.

Timing: 15 minutes

3 Small talk: keeping the conversation going

Introduce the section. Remind students that small talk is always useful:

- at the beginning of a meeting, welcoming a visitor
- at other moments in a business relationship.

Elicit suggestions for:

- during breaks
- meals
- social occasions
- evenings
- moving from one place to another.

Ask what topics are useful for small talk. Remind students that conversation normally arises from the immediate physical environment: the weather, buildings and places, hotels, arrival and departure, meals, the time of day, entertainment, etc. or flows from the conversational context. Write on the board the topics students suggest. Suggest that some subjects are best avoided, but generally there are many which can help to build up personal as well as professional relationships.

In any conversation, the answers to questions and the comments that follow can provide a lead-in to the next comment – or even the next topic – in a conversation. Effective conversation requires that speakers recognise and pick up on these leads. Conversation proceeds on the basis of clues in previous sentences or in the immediate context.

Additional points you may wish to mention:
- small talk helps develop good relations and a good atmosphere
- small talk happens between casual acquaintances, people who meet in the course of their work, perhaps engaged in different fields, or staying in the same hotel or travelling on the same plane.

🔲◉ **1** Following this initial introduction, introduce the recording. Play the first version once. Elicit students' answers to the questions.
a) He doesn't respond to the woman's comment. It appears as if he doesn't care or isn't listening.

Go through the explanation in the Student's Book. Make sure students understand the meaning of *supplementary question*. A supplementary question refers to the *same* topic.

🔲◉ b) Elicit suggestions for a better version of the conversation. Then play the model answer on the recording.

Tapescript

First version

MANAGER: Is this your first visit here?

HEMPER: No, in fact the first time I came was for a trade fair. We began our Southeast Asian operations here at the 2003 Exhibition.

MANAGER: Shall we have a look round the plant before lunch?

Second version

MANAGER: Is this your first visit here?

HEMPER: No, in fact the first time I came was for a trade fair. We began our Southeast Asian operations here at the 2003 Exhibition.

MANAGER: Ah yes, I remember the exhibition well. So it was very successful for you, was it?

HEMPER: Well, we made a lot of useful contacts, not least yourselves.

MANAGER: Of course ... now, shall we have a look round the plant before lunch?

PHOTOCOPIABLE   © Cambridge University Press 2003

---

2 This exercise could be done as self-study or homework.

Key
a) Well, I hope you like it.
b) That's good.
c) Oh, that's a pity. There's such a lot to see.
d) Yes, I'd love to.
e) That's very kind. Thank you.
f) Oh dear, I'm sorry to hear that.
g) What was the problem?
h) Hmm. I hope you didn't feel too bad.

Timing: 15 minutes

🔲◉ **3** Play each extract in turn.
a) i = D, ii = B, iii = A, iv = C.
b) Elicit a range of suggestions from the whole class, allowing some ideas to run for a few sentences, taking contributions from different class members. Occasionally go back to the recording again and repeat, allowing the conversation to take a different course. Here are suggestions for how the conversations might continue:

i) Further questioning on social and political affairs, relations with neighbouring states, next elections, economic conditions for businesses, foreign investment, etc.

ii) Observations on personal leisure preferences, liking for or aversion to exercise / preference for watching rather than doing sport, etc.

iii) Further questioning on the vacation in the States, more detail, reference to one's own visit(s) to the States, opinions, other comments on vacations, preferred types, etc.

iv) Questions about the family, ages of children, partner's work, etc. Discussion of the impact of work on family life.

c) Possible remarks to elicit or suggest include:

i) Depending on the acceptability of political conversation – a difficult area of conversation where some political systems are concerned – the discussion could easily lead to more information and comment on recent changes, future prospects, or refer to personalities involved.

Note: Politics is an interesting area: some foreigners can be baffled by British people's criticism of the British monarchy, for example. Some leaders and some political systems, reviled abroad, may be revered by sections of their own people.

ii) Different cultures have different perceptions of leisure: a drink with friends and associates in a bar can be anathema to some cultures where alcohol is taboo. Likewise, regular physical exercise is not everyone's idea. See also iii.

iii) Leisure activities and holidays in particular may be totally different for different people.

iv) Discussions on family, etc. may be unwelcome between some cultures. Americans or Europeans asking about aspects of family life might be unacceptable to Saudis, for example.

Tapescript

Extract 1

WOMAN: So how are things going generally now, after the recent political changes?

MAN: Much better, I think generally people are more optimistic and the government should be all right now. There's a lot of popular support for government policies.

Extract 2

MAN: I like the thought of sport … it's actually doing it I can't seem to manage. I know I should, you know, keep fit, eat less, go to a gym, use the hotel swimming pool … but somehow I'd rather sit here at the bar and have a chat with whoever comes down. I spend all day working …

Extract 3

MAN: So how do you usually spend your vacations? Do you stay at home or go abroad?

WOMAN: Oh, generally we travel. We were in the States last year, we went to California and to Arizona, we visited a few National Parks …

Extract 4

WOMAN: Well of course, I like working. True, I travel a lot. That's not always so good, because it's difficult for the family. I've got children – they're four and six. My husband, he stays home and looks after them.

Timing: 15 minutes

Practice 2

Have learners work in pairs to talk *non-stop* about the four pictures on page 11 of the Student's Book. Put a time limit on each one. Students should switch immediately to a different picture when you call time.

Fluency exercise option

Develop this exercise, perhaps as a warmer or short fluency exercise at other stages of a lesson, using your own photographs from magazines, or photocopied images projected onto a wall using an OHT.

A variation on this is to use flashcards with various topics on them, such as:

travel	sport	politics / international politics
food	tourism in your country	art, theatre, music

The various topics – or others suggested by the class – are written (or represented in pictures) on flash cards and distributed among the class. Have them stand up and circulate, discussing the topic on one of the cards with anyone in the room. When you call 'change' they have to discuss the other student's topic. When you shout 'change partner' they have to talk to someone else, and so on. Leave two to three minutes between each call.

Timing: 15 minutes

Language Checklist

Students should study the Language and Skills Checklist before practising the role plays on page 11. Tell them that the Language Checklists in the book are usually only a snapshot of all the available alternatives. Check pronunciation and comprehension of what is included. Use this same procedure throughout the book for both Checklists.

Skills Checklist

The Skills Checklist is about preparing for meetings with partners from other countries. It includes suggestions for developing effective cross-cultural understanding and builds on those aspects introduced in the first section of the unit.

Spend a few minutes discussing the recommendations and elicit students' comments and any other suggestions.

Timing: 10 minutes

Role plays

Encourage students to make notes from the Language Checklist if they need to. They should study their role cards for a minute or two, then act out the role play in pairs. The aim is to develop fluency and confidence in handling arrivals and engaging in small talk. You should try to note any problems you hear and refer to them in feedback.

If there is an odd number of students, you should take one of the roles.

Timing: 15 minutes × 2

Role play option

An option is for you to play host or visitor and perform a role play with one or more students in front of the rest of the class. You can throw in added complications and difficulties that learners would probably not include – where's the toilet? (*washroom* in American English), some other difficulties – you need to cancel a hotel booking, hire a car, buy a map, photocopy something, etc.

Transfer

This is an opportunity for students to put the ideas suggested in the Skills Checklist into practice with a specific country in mind. They could work individually, in pairs or in groups. Suggest they use a range of sources for finding out information:

- Published sources
  - books, guidebooks
  - travel information
- Official bodies
  - embassies
  - consulates
  - cultural centres
  - government offices and agents
- Commercial offices
  - travel agents
  - marketing consultants
  - Import and Export offices and agents
- People
  - colleagues who may know the place in question
  - nationals from the country concerned
  - students' own knowledge.

Option

Develop the above into a mini-project for individual or group presentation at a later stage. This could be combined with Module 3 on Presentations.

2 Culture and entertainment

AIMS
- Cross-cultural understanding (2)
- Inviting, and accepting or declining
- Eating out

Briefing

The unit opens with a short reading text designed to emphasise the significance of cultural diversity. Implicit in the text is the warning that working with people from other countries requires an awareness and understanding of differences and that effective partnerships are rarely born out of treating everyone the same.

The rest of the unit covers socialising in a business or professional context. Section 2 comprises talking about social events and making arrangements. Practice activities include writing a letter deferring a social engagement. The final section looks at eating out and making conversation, linking with the section on small talk in the previous unit. There are two role plays, one designed to practise making arrangements, the other set in a restaurant and designed to include functional language in the restaurant context and an opportunity to practise developing small talk.

Language option

The language in this unit covers talking about entertainment options, inviting, accepting and rejecting invitations, language relevant to dining out and small talk. You may choose to focus on the language used once the texts have been dealt with in the ways specifically indicated in the Student's Book.

Role plays

For the role plays, a little planning is necessary. For the first, try to get hold of genuine local materials such as a newspaper or a Tourist Office publication advertising local entertainment. This will require the 'host' to do some explaining for the 'guest'. The same is true for the second role play, set in a restaurant, where using a local menu would be the most realistic approach.

1:1 situation

Naturally you will have to participate in practice exercises and role plays. Do not labour discussion. The language used in the unit is relatively simple. There are many alternatives which could be used equally well. Elicit alternatives and praise appropriate language. Correct as necessary.

Timing: 3 hours

1 Cross-cultural understanding (2)

Referring to the illustration, introduce the concept of cultural diversity. Ensure that it is understood. Ask students what it is that makes people culturally diverse, eliciting a range of features, such as conventions and customs, language, history, religion, historical experience, social systems, geography, regional influences and other features.

1 Have the class read the text once, without attention to detail. Summary B is the best. The other two are, according to the text, wrong.

2 A second reading should enable students to answer the more detailed questions.

Key
  a) They are not 'universal'.
  b) Pay-for-performance has failed in Africa because there are particular unspoken rules

about the sequence and timing of reward and promotions.

c) MBO has generally failed in southern European subsidiaries of multinationals because managers have not wanted to conform to the abstract nature of preconceived policy guidelines.

d) Human-resource management is a typically Anglo-Saxon doctrine that is difficult to translate to other cultures. It borrows from economics the idea that human beings are 'resources' like physical and monetary resources. It assumes individual development. In countries without these beliefs, this concept is hard to grasp and unpopular once understood.

e) International managers' culture of origin, the culture in which they are working, the culture of the organisation employing them.

f) Authority, bureaucracy, creativity, good fellowship, verification and accountability.

Follow up with an explanation of any of the key vocabulary in the text, inviting students' questions. Check that students have understood the text without getting bogged down in wanting to understand absolutely *everything*. Make sure they do not lose sight of the importance of understanding the *main ideas* in a text rather than every *word*.

Option

Spend a few minutes discussing briefly the meaning of the management philosophies referred to in the opening paragraph. Elicit students' ideas and comments before offering your own. Remember that according to Trompenaars they are of little use when applied to different cultures. You may wish to discuss this point further.

Timing: 25 minutes

2 Inviting, and accepting or declining

Elicit ideas in response to the photographs and students' own views on what is likely to provide acceptable local entertainment for professionals visiting their home town. Typical ideas are arts and cultural events such as theatre, cinema, concerts, exhibitions, famous monuments and buildings, or sports events, golf, tourist trips, excursions, restaurants and bars, etc., as well as more private corporate hospitality such as parties, receptions, and possibly invitations to someone's home – though this is highly culture dependent and may be more common in the USA, the UK and some parts of Continental Europe than elsewhere.

1 Play example 1 once and elicit answers to the three questions.
   a) a concert, play or show
   b) a play would be good
   c) the host will find out what is on and call back.

2 Play example 2. Elicit and check the answers given here:
   a) an informal gathering then a meal in a restaurant
   b) accepts with pleasure
   c) they will meet at the hotel at about 7.

Language focus option

Highlight the indirect, very polite invitation in the first example. It allows for the possibility of the visitor declining the invitation.

It is a non-specific invitation expressed in three sentences:
I was wondering if we could fix something up for you when you come? Would you be free on Monday evening? If you like we could do something together?
In the second recording, ask students which sentence offers the visitor a similar opportunity to turn down the invitation. The answer is:
I don't know if you have any other plans this evening?

Tapescript

Example 1

HOST: Well, I was wondering if we could fix something up for you when you come? Would you be free on Monday evening? If you like we could do something together?

VISITOR: That would be very nice, what do you have in mind?

HOST: Well, we could go to see a concert or a play – go to a show, of some kind?

VISITOR: I think the theatre would be interesting. I'd like that.

HOST: Oh, that's good. We'll do that then. I'll find out exactly what's on, then I'll call you.

Example 2

HOST: … and then tonight we've planned a little gathering here, an informal get-together, if you'd like to join us. You'd meet some other colleagues, then we plan to go out to dinner together – a well-known restaurant. I don't know if you have any other plans this evening?

VISITOR: No, not at all. No plans. Well, that sounds like a good combination, talking and eating …

HOST: So, if you like, we'll meet here again at about seven – and take it from there.

VISITOR: Yes, that's perfect.

PHOTOCOPIABLE   © Cambridge University Press 2003

Timing: 15 minutes

📻 ◉ **3** Play the three extracts, one at a time. Elicit the answers below:

1 Activity   opera
Reason for rejection   doesn't like opera
Comments   very direct / sounds rude
2 Activity   dinner party
Reason for rejection   has to return to Zurich
Comments   polite / formal
3 Activity   tennis
Reason for rejection   can't play / wooden leg
Comments   humorous / sarcastic

Tapescript

Extract 1

HOST: There's a very nice opera on at the City Hall tomorrow. If you like, I could book you a ticket. Mozart's *Don Giovanni*.

VISITOR: No, I don't like listening to opera.

HOST: Oh, is there anything you'd like me to fix up for you, a meal in a restaurant?

VISITOR: No, it's okay. It's not necessary.

Extract 2

HOST: We're planning a small party on Saturday, a dinner party. We'd like to invite you, in the evening, I don't know if you can join us?

VISITOR: Er, that would be very nice, I'd like that, but unfortunately I have to return to Zurich the same evening. I'm so sorry about that …

HOST: Oh, dear. That's a shame. Let's hope you can stay longer the next time you come.

VISITOR: Yes, it's a pity, but this time it's impossible …

Extract 3

HOST: So, Viktor, would you like to join us this evening for a game of tennis?

VISITOR: Tennis!? I've got a wooden leg! It's ten years since I played tennis. I think a walk to a restaurant would be enough for me …

HOST: You never know! Tennis could be just what you need.

VISITOR: It would kill me.

PHOTOCOPIABLE   © Cambridge University Press 2003

4 Check on individual pairs, prompting where necessary. Ask for some examples to be given for the whole class to hear. Discourage any writing – it should be spontaneous. Students can use the listings extracts to make their invitations, or use real examples of entertainments on offer locally. You will need to supply a newspaper or guide – it does not have to be in English.

▭◉ Finally, play the recording of model versions and discuss points arising.

Tapescript

Extract 1

INVITATION: Shall we do something together tomorrow night – if you're free? We'd like to invite you to a show or take you round the town a little, or have a meal or something.

ACCEPT: That sounds a good idea. I think I'd like to have a look around the town.

REJECT: That would be nice, but unfortunately I've already made plans for tomorrow night. I plan to visit a friend I haven't seen for some time.

Extract 2

INVITATION: We have arranged a meal in a restaurant this evening. Most of us will be there. Would you like to join us?

ACCEPT: I'd like that very much. Thank you.

REJECT: Er, thank you, but I'll have to say no this time. I have to leave very early tomorrow. I think I'd like an early night.

Extract 3

INVITATION: If you like, we can fix up some entertainment for you. What sort of thing would you like to do while you're here?

ACCEPT: I don't know, what do you recommend? I'd like anything at all, though I'd prefer not to be too late.

REJECT: That's very kind, but I am going to be very busy – I'm not sure I'll have

time. Perhaps we can leave any plans until later.

Timing: 15 minutes

Practice

1 Students should work in pairs to construct a dialogue based on the flow chart. A recording of a model answer is provided, featuring a conversation at the end of the working day between two business associates, one of whom is visiting his partner in Lima, Peru. *Ceviche* is raw fish marinaded in lemon juice.

Tapescript

HOST: Have you tried the local cuisine?

VISITOR: No – not yet, but I've heard it's very good.

HOST: Yes, in particular you should try *ceviche*. Raw fish marinaded in lemon juice.

VISITOR: Hmmm. Sounds interesting! I've heard there are a lot of good local dishes.

HOST: Yes – and we have some very good restaurants. Would you like to visit one? We can try some of these specialities.

VISITOR: Oh, yes, of course, I'd like that very much.

HOST: Right, so do you like fish?

VISITOR: Oh, yes – I do, very much. I've heard that the fish is very special in Lima.

HOST: That's true. So, we'll go to one of the best fish restaurants we've got. Shall I meet you at your hotel this evening?

VISITOR: That'd be good, fine, thank you. What time?

HOST: Er … Shall we say 8.30?

VISITOR: Perfect. Okay, we'll … we'll meet again tonight then.

HOST: Yeah, 8.30 at your hotel. See you there.

VISITOR: Thanks very much. See you later. I'll get back to the hotel now, I'll get a taxi.

HOST: Okay, sure. Bye for now.

Timing: 10 minutes

2   Possible self-study or homework activity. Introduce the email and explain any details that are not clear or any problems in understanding the email.

Here is a model answer to the email reply.

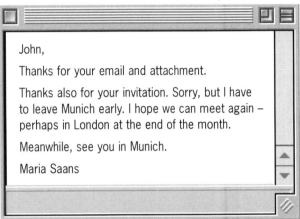

John,

Thanks for your email and attachment.

Thanks also for your invitation. Sorry, but I have to leave Munich early. I hope we can meet again – perhaps in London at the end of the month.

Meanwhile, see you in Munich.

Maria Saans

Option: correspondence

Contrast the brevity of emails with letter correspondence. If you wish, use the examples below to talk about letter-writing conventions, in terms of layout and language. The letters, of course, are more formal than the emails and the style convention more rigorous. Although the letter is formal, the first name is used in the initial salutation after *Dear*. This is common and probably indicates that the writer / addressee use first names on the telephone. Note the opening paragraph in the letter.

Although the letter is formal, but first name is used in the initial salutation after *Dear*. This is common and probably indicates that they already use first names on the telephone. Note too the paragraphing in the letter.

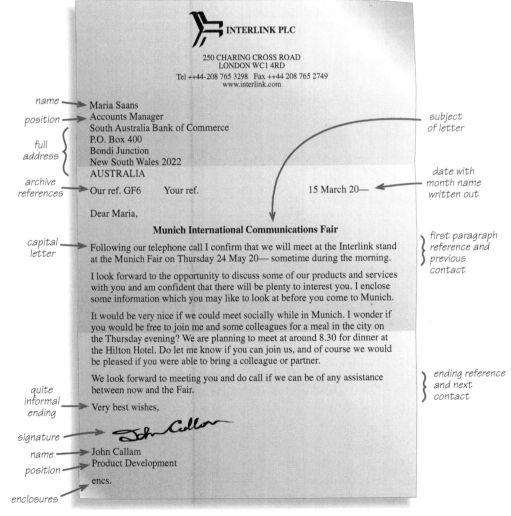

Here is a model answer to John Callam's letter:

South Australia Bank of Commerce

PO Box 400 Bondi Junction New South Wales 2022 AUSTRALIA
Tel. (02) 389 232 Fax. (02) 389 764
www.SABOC.com

John Callam
Product Development
Interlink plc
250 Charing Cross Road
London WC1 4RD

Your ref: GF6   18 March 20—

Dear John,

Munich International Communications Fair

Thank you for your letter of 15 March 20— and thanks also for the
information you sent. I am sure we will have plenty to talk about when
we meet in Munich.

I note your suggestion that we should meet for a meal on Thursday
evening. I would be very pleased to come, but unfortunately on this
occasion I have to decline your invitation as I have to leave Munich
early. However, I will be in London a month later and perhaps we could
meet then. If this idea suits you, we can make arrangements nearer the
time.

In the meantime, I look forward to seeing you as agreed at the
Munich Fair.

Best wishes,

Maria Saans
Accounts Director
m.j.saans.accounts@saboc.co.au

Timing: 20 minutes

Role play 1

This is a simple role play that should require minimal preparation. It will help if you can provide copies of a local 'What's On' guide to entertainment in the area.

Listen to students working and making notes on any language points. Provide feedback for the group as a whole. Choose a couple of pairs to perform their role play before the class.

Timing: 15 minutes

3 Eating out

1 Divide the class into threes and have them brainstorm different phrases for each of the three functions indicated.

2 Once they have done that for five minutes, redivide the class to make new teams of three consisting of individuals from each of the first three groups. Each new group compiles a list of possible phrases to complete the grid.

▭ ◉ **3** Introduce the situation in a New York restaurant. Explain that the recording has four parts. Play the recording once without stopping. Play it again if necessary.

Optional language focus

For weaker students only, play the recording again, stopping it at various points to highlight the functional language. Ask learners to repeat the phrases out loud as you stop the recording. Note that the dialogue is in American English.
appetizer = starter, *check* = bill, *colorful* = colourful, *cab* = taxi

---

Tapescript

PATRICIA:	Let's order ... er ... Can I have a menu, please?
WAITER:	The menu ...
PATRICIA:	Well, it all looks terrific. Shall we have an appetizer?
SANDRA:	Sure, in fact I'm pretty hungry ... oh, I see they have venison on the menu.
PATRICIA:	Oh yeah, the venison's really good.
SANDRA:	Actually, I don't eat a lot of red meat, I'm more of a fish eater.
PATRICIA:	Oh, I'd recommend the fish.
SANDRA:	Great. Well, I'll have the oysters to start.
PATRICIA:	I think I'll have the shrimp. Then why don't we share a mixed seafood grill for two as the main course?
SANDRA:	That would be great. Let's have that ...
PATRICIA:	And wine?
SANDRA:	Well, I prefer white wine, a dry one. Red gives me a headache.
WAITER:	Would you care to order drinks now?
PATRICIA:	Sure, in fact we're ready. To drink we'll try a bottle of Chardonnay, and water, bottled water, please.
WAITER:	Okay, I'll take your food order in just a moment ...
PATRICIA:	So, how does it feel to be back here – it must be a while, a year or two at least ...
PATRICIA:	This looks wonderful ... How are the oysters?
SANDRA:	Just fine. What about the shrimp?
PATRICIA:	Okay, a little spicy.
SANDRA:	It's very busy here.
PATRICIA:	It usually is on Thursdays and on weekends ...
PATRICIA:	You get a lot of business people in here, local and passing through. Ah, here comes the fish grill.
SANDRA:	Oh, it looks fantastic ... what a lot!
PATRICIA:	It's very colourful.
WAITER:	Everything okay with your meal?
SANDRA / PATRICIA:	Perfect / great ...
SANDRA:	That was really great.

PATRICIA:	The check, please.
WAITER:	Here it is, thank you.
SANDRA:	Can I get this?
PATRICIA:	No, no, certainly not, this one's mine.
SANDRA:	Well, okay, thank you. I'll pay next time ... or when you come to Florida. You have to come down soon.
PATRICIA:	I'd really like that. So, what'll we do now?
SANDRA:	I'll get a cab back to the hotel.
PATRICIA:	No, you don't need to do that ... I'll drive you if you want ...
SANDRA:	Oh, that's great ... thanks again.

PHOTOCOPIABLE   © Cambridge University Press 2003

Timing: 30 minutes

Option

File cards 4A and 4B contain menus. There is scope for some discussion and teaching of food and cooking vocabulary here which can be very useful to business people who eat out with business partners. Give simple explanations where necessary for the terms on the menu. In the role play, students have the opportunity to broaden the discussion, to talk about the dishes on the menu and their preferences.

Timing: 20 minutes

Transfer

This Transfer should be set as a self-study or homework activity and could be reviewed in class. Obviously a lot of time could be spent on it but how much effort and time students put into the task should be left up to them as their circumstances and needs dictate.

Skills Checklist

Discuss the usefulness of the recommendations contained in the Skills Checklist for people who need to conduct business across frontiers. Elicit any comments on the Checklist, such as what might be missing from it.

Timing: 10 minutes

3 Could I leave a message?

AIMS	■ Preparing to make a telephone call	■ Asking for and giving repetition
	■ Receiving calls	■ The secretarial barrier
	■ Taking and leaving messages	

Briefing

Many students at intermediate level or below will do everything possible to avoid telephoning in English. For obvious reasons, using the phone has special difficulties.

However, it is worth pointing out three things before beginning this module. Firstly, most of the language used on the telephone in the business context is fairly restricted. There are numerous functions that recur repeatedly in various phone calls. As a result, the language needed in most situations is well within reach of intermediate-level students. The second point is that with increased practice, confidence develops and so does efficient performance. The third is that it is possible to control what happens in a telephone conversation, to ask the caller to call back, to ask for repetition, to ask the other person to speak more slowly, to check and to summarise information.

A recurrent theme throughout the course is that communication activities benefit from good preparation and this preparation should be conducted – as much as possible – in English. The module begins with a section on preparing for a phone call. It is important that students see the value of treating preparation as a vital part of the process of telephoning in English.

A few moments thinking about the call will certainly improve performance. The middle sections of Unit 3 looks at some basic language functions common in phone calls. The final section, The secretarial barrier, is concerned with cold calls.

1:1 situation

The unit works perfectly well with a single student. You will need to take a part in the role plays and Transfer exercises and a more directive role in discussions, eliciting as much as you can but feeding in your own opinions where relevant.

Timing: 3 hours

1 Preparing to make a telephone call

1 Begin by brainstorming on what is required in preparing to make a call. Write students' suggestions on the board. Now let students suggest what the people in the cartoon might be saying to each other. Have students act out the conversation in pairs. Elicit comments on what went wrong and highlight the lack of preparation involved in each situation.

Obviously the caller has not checked the time in Tokyo when it's 11.00 a.m. in New York. There is a time difference of ten hours! Clearly, one should always check times when calling different time zones.

Timing: 5 minutes

⊞ ◉ 2 Introduce the recording of a company director talking about how she prepares to make a telephone call. Students should tick the second, fourth and fifth suggestions. Elicit any other ideas / comments from the class.

- Do not try to guess what the other person will say. *No! You should do this.*
- Think about your objectives from the call –

any questions you need to ask or things you need to say. *Yes.*

- If someone calls and you are not ready for them, ask them to call back later. *No. She does not say this.*
- Desk preparation: prepare the desk – paper, pen, any relevant documentation, computer files. *Yes.*
- Check recent correspondence, know the situation. *Yes.*
- Have your diary on hand, so you can fix appointments. *No. Good advice, but she does not say this.*

Tapescript

CLARE: Well, if I am making a call, prediction is one thing. I have to try to guess what the other person might say – or ask. I think a lot of it is subconscious really – it's a subconscious preparation. But there are more conscious things too, like getting together any information I need, having the right file nearby, my diary, notepaper, a pen and also I might need some particular stuff on the computer screen. All that – what you call desk preparation – is important. Then in addition there's specific things like checking recent correspondence, knowing exactly what's going on – knowing what we ought to be doing – so understanding the situation or the relationship. Then finally, I would say that part of the preparation needs to be – if you're making the call – you have to think about your objectives, what you want from the call, what you may need to ask or need to say. All that should be clear in your mind. So, in conclusion, I'd stress that it's terrible if you're not prepared – it sounds unprofessional and it wastes a lot of time too.

PHOTOCOPIABLE © Cambridge University Press 2003

Timing: 5 minutes

3 Explain how different people have different objectives in a phone call. Ask what students think are the objectives of the people in the

situations below. Talk through the example, then elicit suggestions for the other three situations. Possible answers are given here.

b)
- To talk to someone who can solve the problem.
- To describe the problem and get a solution.

c)
- To find out if Moda Design could be interested in selling his / her products.
- To suggest that he / she sends information or visits Moda Design.

d)
- To defend the company from unsolicited sales calls.
- To get the name of interesting possible new suppliers.
- To give an appointment to possible interesting new suppliers.
- To ask for the names of companies who can speak for new suppliers (references).

Timing: 10 minutes

2 Receiving calls

1 Check that students understand the change of context to incoming calls. Explain that the focus of attention is still on being well prepared.

Although the called person has been caught unawares, he should respond better. Elicit ideas from the class: he could say he's busy just now, get the caller's number and ring back once he has checked what he ought to know.

Tapescript

SPEAKER: Mr Who? Oh yes, about the er … what was it? Oh yes, the er … the contract. You want to know what I think? Did you write to me last week? It was you, wasn't it? Or was it that other company in Geneva?

PHOTOCOPIABLE © Cambridge University Press 2003

2 Introduce a second short extract from the recording of Clare Macey. She is talking

about being prepared for incoming calls. Tick what she recommends.

- Send an email suggesting someone calls you – then be prepared for their call. *No.*
- If you expect a call, think about what the other person will say or what they will ask. *Yes.*
- Check any relevant documentation or correspondence. *Yes.*
- If you are busy or not ready when they call, ask them to call back later. *No, she says offer to call back yourself.*

Tapescript

CLARE: Well, another type of preparation … you can prepare for incoming calls. Of course, you don't always know when someone is going to call, of course not, but you can have some idea just by knowing what work is going on. So, I think … if I know someone's going to call me … then of course it makes sense to think about what they'll be talking about and to try to anticipate what they might ask or say. In other words to predict what might come up – that way I can … er … maybe see if there's anything in particular I need to find out or check before they call – or think about what I need to ask them. So if someone calls me and I'm not really ready to talk to them I often say I'll call back – and I'll ring them when I *am* ready.

PHOTOCOPIABLE © Cambridge University Press 2003

Discuss the appropriacy of the suggestion: it is good advice, but what is a good excuse? Elicit examples: about to start a meeting / someone in the office just now / need to get your file, etc.

Timing: 10 minutes

3 Taking and leaving messages

1 There are four recordings. Deal with each one in turn, playing each one twice. The first time students should simply listen and not feel obliged to write anything. The

second time students should complete the message pad.

Check each message before going on to the next one. After conversations *a* and *b*, discuss the style of the speakers in each one. See *Discussion* below. Then go on to *c* and *d*. Finish by discussing the style in these two as well.

Discussion

Elicit brief comments on the efficiency and politeness of the speakers in calls *a* and *b*. Compare the first example with the style of the (American) caller in the second recording. Throughout the unit there is plenty of opportunity to discuss various styles. Elicit comments on the effectiveness and politeness of the different speakers. In both cases, the 'receptionists' are very polite and efficient and the caller in *a* is extremely helpful, speaking clearly and slowly. The caller in *b* is a contrast, very brief and very direct.

a)

b)
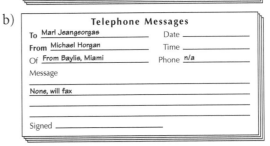

Tapescript

Call a)

MEDIA: Hello, Media Publishing, good morning.

GERDA HOENESS: Oh hello. My name's Gerda Hoeness, from Frankfurt. I'd like to speak to Mr Stefan Pavlov please.

MEDIA: Oh I'm sorry – Mr Pavlov is not here at the moment. Can I er … could I have your name again, please?

GERDA HOENESS: Yes, Gerda Hoeness, that's
G ... E ... R ... D ... A – Gerda
and Hoeness, spelt
H ... O ... E ... N ... E ... S ... S.

MEDIA: Yes, Ms Hoeness, from
Frankfurt?

GERDA HOENESS: That's right. Could you ask him
to call me when he's got a
moment?

MEDIA: Yes, I'll ask him to do that. Does
he have your number?

GERDA HOENESS: Yes, I think so, but in any case
it's 49-69-75-45-22.

MEDIA: I'll repeat that – 49-69-75-45-22.

GERDA HOENESS: Correct.

MEDIA: Okay, thanks for calling. Mr
Pavlov will call you later today.

GERDA HOENESS: Oh, that's very good. Many
thanks.

Call b)

ASSISTANT: Hello, Harris & Co, how can I
help you?

MICHAEL: Hi, Michael Horgan here from Baylis
in Miami. Is Mari Jeangeorges there?

ASSISTANT: I beg your pardon? Who would you
like to speak to?

MICHAEL: Mari Jeangeorges? Is she there?

ASSISTANT: Who's calling, please?

MICHAEL: Michael Horgan.

ASSISTANT: I'm sorry, Mrs Jeangeorges has
already left the office today. Shall I ask
her to call you tomorrow?

MICHAEL: No, it's okay. I'll send her an email.

ASSISTANT: Oh, okay. That'll be fine. Do you have
her address?

MICHAEL: Yeah, no problem. I'll email her. Bye
for now.

ASSISTANT: Bye.

PHOTOCOPIABLE © Cambridge University Press 2003

c) Introduce recording *c* as a call to Altona
Helpline, a customer service department
for a computer software company.
Play the recording twice, the first time
asking two general questions. First, what
kind of a call is this? *Formal, request for
assistance.*

What do you think is the relationship
between the people involved? *Formal,
business – they do not know each other.*
Play the conversation again. Get students to
complete the message pad as shown below:

c)

d) Introduce extract *d* as a call to the
Computer Services Helpdesk in a large
company. The first time, ask two general
questions:
Is the caller ringing from inside the
company? Is it formal or informal?
Internal, informal.
What do you think is the relationship
between the people involved?
*Though they work for the same company,
they probably don't know each other very
well.*
During the second listening, students
should complete the message pad.
Here is the completed message pad:

d)

Discussion

The called person in *c* is very service-minded. In
d, there is a contrast, as Angela sounds totally
bored and disinterested. The caller clearly is not
getting satisfaction. Point out how Angela uses no

'active listening', making no response, giving no repetition or encouragement. Elicit ways in which she could have been better.

Timing: 30 minutes

Tapescript

Call c)

TOMASINA:	Hello, my name's Tomasina Harks, thank you for calling Altona, how may I help you?
JOHN:	Hello, my name's John Curly, that's C … U … R … L … Y, John Curly. I'd like to speak to Fred Roper, if I may.
TOMASINA:	Okay, well I'm sorry, but Fred's on another call just now. Can I take a message or perhaps I can help you?
JOHN:	Yes, please. Could you tell him that I called – the email he sent me arrived but there should have been an attachment. It came with no attachment, so can he resend the email with the attachment? Perhaps also he could send the document by regular mail because it could be a problem for me to read what he sends.
TOMASINA:	Sure. Does he have your address?
JOHN:	No, I'd better give it to you. The email address, yes, he has that. The postal address is Auto Matrix, 270 James Road, Stretford Road East, Manchester MU16 1DY, England.
TOMASINA:	Let me check that. John Curly, Auto Matrix, 217 …
JOHN:	No, 270, two seven zero, James Road.
TOMASINA:	Right, okay, *270* James Road, then did you say Stratford Road?
JOHN:	No, Stretford, S … T … R … E … T … F … O … R … D, Stretford Road *East*, Manchester.
TOMASINA:	MU16 1DY.
JOHN:	Correct.
TOMASINA:	Okay, may I have your phone number too?
JOHN:	Yes, its 0161 399 5576.
TOMASINA:	Right, thanks. I'll get the message to him and he'll do that today.
JOHN:	Thank you very much. Goodbye.
TOMASINA:	Goodbye.

Call d)

ANGELA:	Hello.
PAUL:	Computer Services?
ANGELA:	Yes.
PAUL:	It's Paul Maley here from Product Support. I've a problem with the email on my machine. Er … I've been trying to send a document file to Italy and I keep getting the message back that it's been returned. Returned mail. (*pause*) I don't understand why. (*pause*) The colleague in Italy asked me about FTP … File Transfer Protocol? I don't know if we have that. I was trying to send my document as an attachment … er … but it hasn't worked … hello?
ANGELA:	Yeah … what? Italy, you said?
PAUL:	Yes. What about this FTP … what … why do you think it isn't working?
ANGELA:	Just a minute. I've just got to talk to someone here … wait a minute … (*pause*) I'll get Alex to call you back sometime this afternoon. What's your number?
PAUL:	What? It's 6681. Listen … this is urgent …

PHOTOCOPIABLE   © Cambridge University Press 2003

Language focus option

Note: The language of 'getting through' is not overtly examined in the Student's Book. However, since there are several examples of requesting a particular person, you may wish to focus on these. Ask learners what the response would be if the person were available.

Hold on, please,
Who shall I say is calling,
One moment, please,
I'll put you through,
Hold the line, please, etc.

You may also choose to focus on some of the language in the recordings by asking learners to repeat certain phrases, to write them down if they are not sure about them, etc.

Practice

Learners may write the dialogue based on the given flow chart or use it as a skeleton for practice in pairs or with you. Remind them that the language they have heard is typical of what is required here. There is a recording of a model answer.

Timing: 15 minutes

Tapescript

RECEPTION:	Good morning, Gorliz and Zimmerman.
LARA CAMDEN:	Hello, my name's Lara Camden from Bulmer Cables Ltd. Please could I speak to Mr Conrad Bird?
RECEPTION:	I'm sorry, but Mr Bird is not in at the moment.
LARA CAMDEN:	I see. Er … when do you think I could contact him?
RECEPTION:	Well, at the moment he's away. Would you like to leave a message?
LARA CAMDEN:	Yes, perhaps you would ask Mr Bird to call me? My name's Camden, Lara Camden, on 020 8299 462.
RECEPTION:	020 8299 462. Lara Canden. Okay?
LARA CAMDEN:	Er… Camden. C … A … M … D … E … N.
RECEPTION:	Oh yes, sorry! I've got that now.
LARA CAMDEN:	Thank you. I look forward to hearing from Mr Bird.
RECEPTION:	It's a pleasure. Thanks for calling. Bye for now.
LARA CAMDEN:	Goodbye.

PHOTOCOPIABLE © Cambridge University Press 2003

4 Asking for and giving repetition

▭ ◎ **1** Introduce the recording as a conversation between a Malaysian woman who calls the Human Resources office of an American company, Michigan Insurance Inc. She has to attend for a job interview for a position in a new office in Kuala Lumpur.

a) After the first listening students should just say why she calls.
- She has to change the date of her appointment. She wrote, but she has not had a reply.

b) Play the recording again. Students have to identify the reasons for the four requests for repetition:
- wants caller to repeat her name
- asks for spelling
- did not hear who the caller wrote to
- wants to check that he has got the dates right (he had not).
  Note that in the last example, he checks his understanding by paraphrasing (repeating) what the caller said.

▭ ◎ **2** Now go on to highlight the usual structure of requests for repetition. Tell the students that each time there is a request for repetition, the person asking for the repetition also acknowledges it, or asks another question. Highlight this structure through the example given.

Then play the conversation again, asking students to identify two other ways to acknowledge repetition.
- I see.
- Right. I've got that now.
  Elicit and / or discuss other alternatives, such as *Okay, I understand, Thank you*, or straightforward repetition of the name, number, spelling, etc.

Timing: 20 minutes

Tapescript

RECEPTIONIST:	Good morning. Michigan Insurance, how can I help you?
KIT-MEE LEUNG:	Hello. My name is Kit-Mee Leung. I recently wrote to you about an interview date, but I haven't had any reply.
RECEPTIONIST:	I'm sorry, could you repeat your name, please?
KIT-MEE LEUNG:	Yes. Leung. Kit-Mee Leung.
RECEPTIONIST:	Can you spell that, please.

KIT-MEE LEUNG:	L ... E ... U ... N ... G. Leung. And Kit-Mee is K ... I ... T ... hyphen M ... E ... E.
RECEPTIONIST:	I see. And who did you write to?
KIT-MEE LEUNG:	To Mr Malley in Human Resources.
RECEPTIONIST:	I beg your pardon – I didn't catch that.
KIT-MEE LEUNG:	To Allan P. Malley, or Malley – Human Resources Department.
RECEPTIONIST:	Oh yes. Did you suggest an interview date?
KIT-MEE LEUNG:	Originally I had a date for May 12 but I had to ask you to change it. I wrote requesting any day between May 14 and 17.
RECEPTIONIST:	So – you could not come on May 12 – you asked for May 14 or 17?
KIT-MEE LEUNG:	Not exactly. I asked for any day between May 14 and 17.
RECEPTIONIST:	OK. I've got that now. Could you hold on, please?

▭ ◎ **3** Students should look at the illustrations while you play the extracts. Ask students to suggest why someone might ask for repetition and suggest a suitable phrase.

Picture 1
- Unfamiliarity of foreign name.
- Sorry, could you spell that, please?

Picture 2
- Too many numbers spoken too rapidly, with a noisy environment.
- I'm sorry, I didn't catch the dimensions. Can you repeat them more slowly?

Picture 3
- Technical information given to a non-specialist.
- Sorry, I don't understand. (Can you explain that?)

Tapescript

Call 1

A: Who shall I say is calling, please?

B: Theodor Phylaxeos from Boston, Massachusetts.

Call 2

C: So the dimensions have to be 225 by 45 by 3.5 and for the other one 125 by 50 by 5.5 and we need 240 of the first and 180 of the others. Did you get that?

Call 3

D: They're registered shares with restricted transferability.

Timing: 10 minutes

Role plays 1 and 2

Using role plays in the telephoning module

As with other role plays, you may wish to record conversations. However, it is perhaps more important to listen to students' own observations on what problems they have had and to offer some selective feedback based on what you have noted as you listen. Decide if some or all of the students should perform their conversation for the rest of the group to hear.

With telephoning practice, of course, the ideal is a telephone link between two rooms. Teaching telephones are perfect and you should use them if you can as they lend authenticity to the practice exercises. Alternatively, and at the very least, sit pairs of students back to back so they cannot see each other.

Role plays 1 and 2 are designed to practise taking messages in a situation where both sides are keen to be as helpful as possible.

Timing: 15 minutes

5 The secretarial barrier

Discuss the implications of the cartoon introducing this section. Ask students about their experience of dealing with hostile secretaries or if they themselves have ever performed a similar role.

One implication is that here is a company that does not want to do business!

▭ ◎ **1** Introduce the recording by discussing the term 'cold call'. Who makes such calls and why? Introduce the situation in the recording, explaining who Dominique Peron is. Play the recording once, asking students to say what Dominique is trying to do.

Key

a) The Personal Assistant does not want the caller to talk to her boss – she puts him off.

b) She finally suggests he sends information about his products.

2 Play the recording again, stopping the tape at the relevant points to give students time to write down the phrases used by Dominique Peron to block the caller. These are highlighted in the script below.

Tapescript

CTG: Bonjour, ici la CTG.

WALTER BARRY: Good morning, Walter Barry, here, calling from London. Could I speak to M. Le Grand, please?

CTG: Who's calling, please?

WALTER BARRY: I'm sorry – Walter Barry, from London.

CTG: Er, **what is it about**, please?

WALTER BARRY: Well, I understand that your company has a chemical processing plant. My own company, LCP, Liquid Control Products, is a leader in safety in the field of chemical processing. I would like to speak to M. Le Grand to discuss ways in which we could help CTG protect itself from problems and save money at the same time.

CTG: Yes, I see. Well, M. Le Grand **is not available just now**.

WALTER BARRY: Can you tell me when I could reach him?

CTG: He's **very busy for the next few days** – then **he'll be away** in New York. So it is difficult to give you a time.

WALTER BARRY: Could you ask him to ring me?

CTG: I **don't think I could do that** – he's **very busy just now**.

WALTER BARRY: Could I speak to someone else, perhaps?

CTG: Who in particular?

WALTER BARRY: A colleague, for example?

CTG: You are speaking to his Personal Assistant. I can deal with calls for M. Le Grand.

WALTER BARRY: Yes, well … er … yes … could I ring him tomorrow?

CTG: No, **I'm sorry he won't be free tomorrow**. Listen, let me suggest something. You send us details of your products and services, together with references from other companies and then we'll contact you.

WALTER BARRY: Yes, that's very kind. I have your address.

CTG: Very good, Mr … er … er …

WALTER BARRY: Barry. Walter Barry from LCP in London.

CTG: Right, Mr Barry. We look forward to hearing from you.

WALTER BARRY: Thank you. Goodbye.

CTG: Bye.

Timing: 15 minutes

Discussion

Elicit comments on how Dominique Peron handles the caller. She could be complimented for carrying out her brief competently – she certainly shields her boss. But isn't she a little rude (she consistently forgets the caller's name)? If she really thinks it is okay for the caller to send information about his products, she could have suggested this at the beginning and not wasted so much time. If not, she should not have suggested it but merely said 'Thanks for your call, but we are happy with our present systems and suppliers' – if she really is sure that that is the case.

The caller could have asked permission to send some documentation about his products and tentatively floated the idea of a subsequent meeting. He could have tried to speak to someone other than the Production Controller.

Timing: 5 minutes

▭ ◉ **3** Introduce the next conversation. Play the recording once and elicit students' comments and answers.

Key

a) The service department.

b) He gets through and learns some useful information (the name of equipment the prospect already uses).

c) He is successful because he asks for a department or section, not an individual. He wants to get in touch with users of the relevant equipment. He is more interested in talking to users at this stage than actual purchasers or senior management.

Timing: 5 minutes

Tapescript

FUMI AUTO:	Good morning. Fumi Auto Limited.
CALLER:	Hello. Could I have the service department please?
FUMI:	One moment, please. I'll put you through.
SERVICE DEPT.:	Hello, Service.
CALLER:	Hello. I'm calling about precision measuring equipment. My company produces precision measuring instruments and I wonder if you have any problems with precision measuring of any kind. For example, could you tell me what equipment you presently use?
SERVICE DEPT.:	Well, certainly we do use that kind of equipment, we've got a PT200, we've had it for a number of years now …

PHOTOCOPIABLE © Cambridge University Press 2003

Role plays 3 and 4

These very short (two to three minutes only) role plays are designed to practise the cold call situation, where the caller is making an unsolicited approach to a potential customer. In each case, the customer (or prospect) is not really interested in being cooperative. As before, provide and elicit feedback.

Timing: 15 minutes

Transfer

Students should work in pairs, A and B. Each student assumes role A as deviser and planner of a situation relating to his / her interests. In the interaction phase, one student adopts a secondary role, B, role playing a part in a situation devised by the other learner, A.

Once completed, students turn their attention to the other situation and switch roles A and B.

1 Devise situations. Students both assume role A to plan and devise a task relating to their own work, interests or choices. In most cases they are *themselves* in the envisaged interaction task.

2 Selection. Students decide whose situation to perform first.

3 Joint planning phase. The deviser and planner (A) explains the situation and the other role to his / her partner (B). Discussion and clarification ensues.

4 Interaction phase. Partners A and B perform A's situation. A is simulating himself / herself in a real situation, B is role playing, for example as a receptionist.

5 Feedback.

6 Switch roles A and B. Perform other learner's situation following the same steps.

The teacher's role is to supervise the planning phases, especially to ensure that B is clear on his / her role. Encourage B to produce unexpected complications so that the actual interaction phase contains surprises and the need on A's part to genuinely respond to what B says.

If possible record the conversations or at the very least make notes to help you to provide positive and negative feedback.

Skills Checklist

Discuss the Checklist with students and elicit any other points which they may find useful when preparing for a call. In this way, the exercise can serve as a summary of the material covered in the unit.

Timing: 10 minutes

4 Good to hear from you again!

AIMS	■ Cross-cultural communication on the telephone (1)	■ Changing arrangements
	■ Making arrangements	■ Ending a call

Briefing

This includes work on telephoning technique and looks at some cross-cultural considerations, vital for telephoning across international frontiers. This is further developed in Unit 5.

The language work builds on the foundations established in Unit 3 and looks at making arrangements. The unit also includes recommendations concerning the end of a call.

1:1 situation

You will need to take a part in the role plays and Transfer exercises and have a more directive role in discussions, eliciting as much as you can but feeding in your own opinions where relevant.

Timing: 3 hours

1 Cross-cultural communication on the telephone (1)

■◎ **1** Play each extract in turn, with a brief discussion after each one to check students' answers to the matching exercise, identification of the problem in each case and suggested solutions.

Key

Conversation 1 Picture b
Problem
    The person receiving the call speaks only Japanese.
Solution
    The caller should have sent a fax first to say when he would call and indicate the reason for calling.

Conversation 2 Picture c
Problem
    The caller obviously speaks English very well, but uses a metaphor – very difficult for most non-native speakers to understand.
Solution
    International English tends to avoid use of complex metaphors.

Conversation 3 Picture a
Problem
    One side is incredibly unforthcoming – no active listening. This sounds disinterested and rude.
Solution
    Active listening supports the speaker with expressions which indicate interest and understanding, like *Yes, okay, right*, etc. Elicit other examples.

Tapescript

Conversation 1
KYOTO: XXXXXXXXXXXXX
GALLO: Hello, Michael Piccolo, here, calling from New York. Could I speak to someone in Exports, please?
KYOTO: XXXXXXXXXXXXX
GALLO: I beg your pardon? Could you speak English, please?
KYOTO: XXXXXXXXXXXXX
GALLO: Hello? Is there anyone there who speaks English?
KYOTO: XXXXXXXXXXXXX
GALLO: Oh dear. Er … I'll call again later.

Conversation 2

A: Yes, I think we have a little difficulty here. I think we're barking up the wrong tree.

B: I beg your pardon?

A: I said we're barking up the wrong tree.

B: Sorry, I don't understand.

A: We're wasting our time going for that market.

B: Okay, I think … I think I understand … the wrong tree?

A: Yes, the wrong market.

Conversation 3

AMBO: Ambo Computers.

MARIA: Hello, Marie Eckstein, here. I'm calling about my computer, a CX3000. I left it to be repaired last week and you couldn't tell me when it would be ready – We weren't sure what the problem was and er… I was to phone to find out. Is it ready? Can you tell me anything about it? Hello? Are you still there?

AMBO: Yes, I'm here. … What did you say your name was?

Timing: 15 minutes

2 Remind students of the recommended procedure for dealing with reading texts in the book: look at the text, then read it quickly without trying to understand every word. *If necessary*, read parts (or the whole text) in more detail after that. See the section in the Introduction on reading texts, page v.

Key

a) Telephoning people with different cultural backgrounds from yourself.

b) To show how people understand the same words differently – literally or more metaphorically.

c) Elicit comments or suggestions from learners, including: keeping things clear, simple, direct, respecting other people's cultural differences.

3 Now students should read the text. Get them to identify the points asked for.

Key

a) Good preparation.

b) Speak slowly, clearly and use simple language.

c) Repeat what you have understood, look for confirmation, ask for repetition if necessary.

d) North America, Scandinavia, Germany and France are 'explicit' countries – direct talking, making it quite clear what they mean.

e) Japanese, Russians and Arabs – a more indirect style of talking, so more difficult to interpret what they think.

f) You cannot see the body language.

As a follow-up, refer to the comment on how the British talk on the phone (presence of 'small talk' at the beginning and end of the call). Ask if students are used to this in their own cultures.

In general, encourage any discussion arising from the exercise. Ask if points about different countries, including the issue of 'small talk', surprise the learners or conform to their expectations and / or experience. You might allow a brief diversion into talking about national stereotypes. Identify any in the text.

4
Key

1 literal	a)	direct and clear
2 understatement	b)	less strong way of talking
3 deduce	b)	work out
4 vague	a)	unclear
5 devious	b)	dishonest
6 pleasantries	c)	polite remarks

Ask students to look at the cartoon on page 36. The point here is that the language people use can easily lead to the wrong interpretation. The man's typically English understatement 'Not so bad' is understood to mean 'terrible'. Her response is the opposite, giving him an impression that is very positive. The lesson here is to think about how the other person will understand what you say.

Timing: 20 minutes

2 Setting up appointments

📼 ◎ **1** Introduce the extract as a call between two colleagues, Lara and Bob, needing to discuss a personnel problem. Another colleague, Leon, has resigned. Students should write the details of the appointment in the diary.

- Meeting with Lara at 9.00 a.m. Thursday.

Tapescript

LARA: Bob? Lara here. Listen, Bob. I really think we should meet to work out what to do about replacing Leon, we have to find someone.

BOB: Okay, when? When do you mean?

LARA: Now, if you like.

BOB: No, no – I can't right now – I've a meeting with Ravesi. A difficult one … er … might take all day. Tomorrow. It'll have to be tomorrow – or late today?

LARA: No, no, tomorrow's okay. You'll come here?

BOB: Yeah, I'll come to you – say 9 o'clock?

LARA: Right, okay, we'll meet in the morning, at 9.00.

BOB: Okay. Bye then.

LARA: See you.

PHOTOCOPIABLE   © Cambridge University Press 2003

📼 ◎ **2** Introduce the situation: Vladimir Kramnik from Moscow calls Swallow Exports for an appointment with Ms Hannam. Students should write the arrangements made in Ms Hannam's diary.

Key

June 5th, evening: meal with Mr Kramnik.
June 6th, morning: meeting with Mr Kramnik.

Tapescript

RECEPTIONIST: Good morning, Swallow Exports, how can I help you?

VLADIMIR: Hello, Vladimir Kramnik calling from Moscow. I wrote to Ms Hannam last week and she sent me an email suggesting I called to make an appointment … for me to visit her in London. We need to discuss the renewal of a distribution contract.

RECEPTIONIST: Oh yes, I'll put you through to Ms Hannam's secretary. Hold the line, please.

SECRETARY: Hello, Mr Kramnik. Thanks for calling. Now, when would suit you?

VLADIMIR: Well, in fact I can come almost any time next month, and probably towards the end of a week would suit me best.

SECRETARY: I see. Well, how about the week beginning June 24th? Ms Hannam is away during the middle of the month, so either the end of June or the first week of July would be best.

VLADIMIR: Well, could we make it earlier then? I mean – early in June? How about the week beginning the 3rd?

SECRETARY: Let me see … Could we say Thursday 6th?

VLADIMIR: Yes, that's alright. What time shall I come?

SECRETARY: Well, would you plan to arrive in London that day, or come the night before and stay in a hotel?

VLADIMIR: Oh, I think it would be better to arrive the night before and meet early in the day. Then I think I'd plan to leave the same day.

SECRETARY: Well, I'm sure Ms Hannam would like to meet you for dinner on the Wednesday evening, so …

VLADIMIR: That would be very nice.

SECRETARY: Well, shall I send you an email confirming this, then you can send me your flight details. Oh, and I'll … I'll fix you a hotel in the centre of London and send you details of that, too.

VLADIMIR: Oh, thank you very much, that's very kind.

SECRETARY: Not at all. Is that everything?

VLADIMIR:	Yes, I think so. I look forward to your email. You have my email address?
SECRETARY:	Yes, of course. Thank you very much for calling, Mr Kramnik. We look forward to seeing you next month.
VLADIMIR:	Thank you. Goodbye.
SECRETARY:	Goodbye, Mr Kramnik.

3
Key

a) Suggests dinner on Wednesday evening, confirms everything by email and arranges a hotel for Wednesday night.

b) They are extremely service-minded, helpful and polite. Formal and correct, but very efficient.

c) Elicit comments on the styles of the two conversations. Look for the information below:

- The first is much more informal. It is a conversation between colleagues in the same company. They use first names, direct forms: *I really think we should … / Okay, when? When do you mean? / Now if you like / No, I can't …* etc.

- The second is obviously between partners working in different companies – the caller wants to discuss a (distribution) contract. Swallow Exports is evidently a fairly large company. The conversation is always very polite and quite formal, using family names and a more indirect style. There are various polite phrases which typify a formal service-minded approach.

… how can I help you?
Hold the line, please.
Thanks for calling. Now, when would suit you?
Could we say Thursday 6th? Would that be okay?
Well I'm sure Ms Hannam would like to meet you for dinner on the Wednesday evening so …
Well, shall I send you an email confirming this, then you can send me your flight details.
Thank you very much for calling, Mr Kramnik.
We look forward to seeing you next month.

You may also refer back to Section 5, The secretarial barrier, in Unit 3. Contrast the different styles used in this unit with that employed by M. Le Grand's Personal Assistant.

Timing: 15 minutes

Language option

If you think it is appropriate, spend more time on the actual language, targeting the italicised phrases above, which typify the service-minded approach. Use the tape and the pause button to highlight them, getting learners to repeat them.

Practice 1

Explain the background to the conversation outlined in the flow chart. Either work through the flow chart with the whole class eliciting suitable phrases or have students work in pairs to do the same. Then have two or three pairs perform the conversation for the class to hear.

Offer feedback after each pair.

There is a recording of a model example of the conversation.

Timing: 12 minutes

Tapescript

INTERSHIP:	Intership, good morning.
COMPUTECH:	Hello, my name's Alex Hall from Computech Arcos in Singapore.
INTERSHIP:	Sorry, did you say Alex Hall from Computech Arcos?
COMPUTECH:	Yes, that's right.
INTERSHIP:	Okay, how can I help you, Mr Hall?
COMPUTECH:	Well, I'd like an appointment with Mr Dionis.
INTERSHIP:	Can you tell me what it's about?
COMPUTECH:	Certainly. I'd like to discuss the transporting of goods from Singapore to Athens.
INTERSHIP:	I see. When would be a good time for you to come here?
COMPUTECH:	May I suggest next week?
INTERSHIP:	I'm sorry, next week's not possible – Mr Dionis is away next week. How about the beginning of next month?

COMPUTECH: Yes, that would be okay. Could we say Monday, 3rd of May?

INTERSHIP: Er, unfortunately, Mr Dionis is busy all day on that Monday. He could make it Tuesday 4th.

COMPUTECH: That's fine. Shall we say 10.00 a.m.?

INTERSHIP: Yes, that's a good time for us. Er … can I ask you to confirm by email? And would you like us to book you a hotel?

COMPUTECH: I'll email you – and, thank you, but no, the hotel booking isn't necessary. I think that's everything, for now.

INTERSHIP: Right, many thanks, we look forward to your email to confirm the meeting. Goodbye, Mr Hall.

COMPUTECH: Bye for now.

Practice 2

Discuss why companies often use the fax together with the telephone. Suggested uses of the fax are:

- to advise that one is going to phone at a stated time
- to send details that might be misunderstood on the phone
- to send technical information
- to send informal messages to someone who is not there
- to save time
- to confirm arrangements or details of something
- to send information which has to be read quickly before discussion – often on the telephone.

Ask students to use the given template to write a fax confirming the arrangements made in the above conversation. This is a suitable homework or self-study exercise.

Here is a model answer:

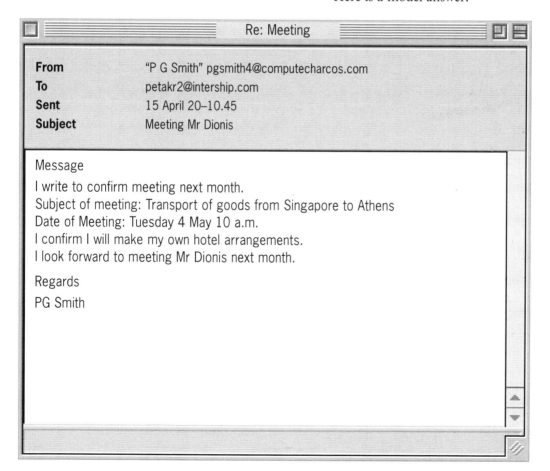

Re: Meeting

From	"P G Smith" pgsmith4@computecharcos.com
To	petakr2@intership.com
Sent	15 April 20–10.45
Subject	Meeting Mr Dionis

Message
I write to confirm meeting next month.
Subject of meeting: Transport of goods from Singapore to Athens
Date of Meeting: Tuesday 4 May 10 a.m.
I confirm I will make my own hotel arrangements.
I look forward to meeting Mr Dionis next month.

Regards
PG Smith

Timing: 10 minutes

3 Changing arrangements

▭ ◉ **1** Introduce the conversation on the recording between two colleagues, John and Pamela. Elicit answers to the introductory questions:

Key

a) 4 o'clock today.
b) Something has happened and so John has to go home early.
c) They will have a 'working lunch' together on Thursday at 12.30.

2 If necessary, play the recording again to confirm the above, but also asking students to note the style of the conversation. Elicit the following:

Key

a) Very informal, very colloquial.
b) Friends and colleagues, native English speakers.

▭ ◉ **3** Play the extract again. This time ask students to follow the four-part structure of a conversation about changing arrangements and to complete the missing words from the given phrases.

Make sure the four-part structure is clear.

(1) Reference to original arrangement
'We're *supposed to meet today* ... '
|
(2) Statement of problem → Need for change
'I'm *sorry*, I really can't *make it.*'
|
(3) Fixing new appointment
'Can we *meet some other time?*'
etc.
|
(4) Confirmation
'See you *Thursday, then.*'

Tapescript

JOHN: Hello, it's John, Pamela. Listen, I'm sorry Pamela, we're supposed to meet at 4 o'clock today about the trip to Riyadh next month. Um ... I'm sorry, I really

can't make it, something's happened and I've got to go home early. Can we meet some other time, perhaps?

PAMELA: Just a minute, I'll look at my calendar ... yes, well ... Wednesday ... I've got a meeting in the morning – we won't need too long, will we? It's only to talk about a few general ideas ... can we meet over lunch? You know, have a working lunch ... ?

JOHN: Yes, I guess that'd be fine. I'll come up to you at about 12.30.

PAMELA: Fine, okay. Oh, wait a minute ... there is something ... I've got to go out tomorrow for lunch ... can we make it Thursday?

JOHN: Thursday? Yes, okay – 12.30. See you Thursday then.

PAMELA: Great. See you later.

JOHN: Okay, thanks.

Timing: 15 minutes

Role play 1

Students should work in pairs, A and B. Allow a couple of minutes' preparation before carrying out the role plays with all pairs working simultaneously. Take notes to provide feedback. Depending on the class, you may choose to have students perform their role plays.

The role play is about fixing a meeting with someone from a different company – a client / customer relationship. Remind students of the sorts of considerations they should make in preparing for such a telephone call.

Timing: 10 minutes

Role play 2

Students should keep to the same roles A and B. This exercise is to rearrange the agreement made in the first role play. Follow the same procedure as above, with different students performing in front of the class.

Timing: 10 minutes

4 Ending a call

1 Explain that students will listen to a recording of Catherine Welsh, a Communications Consultant, talking about telephoning and, in particular, ending calls. But tell them that before they hear what she says, you want them to think about possible solutions to the problems. Have them work in pairs to suggest ideas. Do not examine their answers yet.

Key

a) Repeat details, confirm agreements, send a fax.

b) *Is that all?* or *Anything else?*

c) Small talk helps to build and maintain friendly relationships – but keep it brief!

d) Make a polite excuse, say you have a meeting, offer to call back later.

2 Now introduce the recording. Students should compare Catherine's suggestions with their own, adding any new suggestions she makes. Elicit answers and comments on this and the previous question.

Tapescript

CATHERINE: Well, on the phone, you need to check everything – or a lot of things – to avoid misunderstandings. You should repeat details, specifications, times, spellings, dates, all that sort of thing. Prices, even. And if you make agreements, you should confirm them. I think it's best to end calls with some sort of check or confirmation. You might even ask for a fax confirmation.

MAN: Yes, that's quite common. What else would you include in the end of a phone call?

CATHERINE: Well, there's checking that there's nothing left to say. How many times does it happen that you put the phone down and then say 'Oh I forgot to say such and such' or 'I meant to ask about something else'.

You have to phone back – it's such a waste of time. You can usually avoid that if one of you says something like 'Is that all?' or 'Anything else?'

MAN: Okay. And do you think the business phone call is strictly about business?

CATHERINE: Well, in a sense, yes. Small talk can be very important – and it is all business. There's usually a bit of small talk in phone calls, even if it's just a comment on the weather – or how someone is, or your last trip away. It's easy to underestimate the importance of small talk … you have to learn to feel confident with it.

MAN: Why do you think small talk is so important?

CATHERINE: Well, it helps to build and maintain relationships. There are dangers though – it should be kept brief!

MAN: And how do you get off the phone when the other side is talking about the weather for ages … and you don't want to be rude?

CATHERINE: Oh, yes. That can be difficult. I think it's best to interrupt politely, say you have to go somewhere. You can say 'Er, yes, we'll have to talk again soon. I really had better go now, I've a meeting in five minutes', or something like that. If it's a customer, you can offer to call back later if there's anything else to discuss.

PHOTOCOPIABLE   © Cambridge University Press 2003

Timing: 10 minutes

3 Explain the situation: Hans Rossler is in his office in Munich. He is on the phone to Hassam Akhtar from Morocco, who is planning to visit him. Students will hear two versions of how Hans ends the same conversation. Play the recording of both endings once. Ask students to listen, and say
a) what is wrong in the first version, and
b) which key phrase is in the second ending that was not in the first one.

Key

    a) Too abrupt: no check that Hassam has nothing else to say / ask. Also, doesn't end with the polite phrase *look forward to seeing you.*

    b) Anything else you need to know?

Give students the opportunity to suggest why, in most cases, the first type of ending is not so good. Possible reasons: not so friendly and helpful – so may give a wrong impression; no confirmation, no check that the person planning to visit knows exactly what to do – so he may make a mistake; does not give the opportunity to ask more questions – may mean they have to call again – waste of time / money.

Tapescript

Ending 1

HANS: Right, then Hassam, that's good. We'll talk about the possible new price structure when you come. See you in Munich. You have all the information you need. Goodbye.

Ending 2

HANS: Right, then, Hassam, that's good. We'll talk about the possible new price structure when you come. See you in Munich. You have all the information you need … er … I think. Anything else you need to know? Yes, when you get to Munich, you get the S-bahn to the Hauptbahnhof, it's easy. The hotel's right next to the station. Okay, look forward to seeing you in Munich. Bye.

Timing: 10 minutes

    4 Introduce the recording of a conversation between two colleagues, Celia Walton and Gerd Hoffmann.

Key

    a) Celia wants to cut the conversation, but Gerd keeps talking.

    b) She finally interrupts him and suggests calling him another time, perhaps later in the week, or he can call her.

Language focus option

You may like to focus on the attempts she makes to get away from the conversation. Stop the tape and ask students to repeat the phrases:

- … I've a meeting in a little while …
- Yes. Gerd, I'll ring you another time, perhaps this week, or you call me if there's any problems. Okay?

Tapescript

GERD: Yes, but then do you know what happened? It was snowing! Can you believe it? It was actually snowing and there I was at 8 o'clock at night, outside the office, trying to load the van …

CELIA: Yes, I'm sure … I've a meeting in a little while …

GERD: So, everything was getting wet, I was freezing, and then guess who arrived, just when I was about finished?

CELIA: Yes. Gerd, I'll ring you another time, perhaps this week, or you call me if there are any problems. Okay?

GERD: You've got to go?

CELIA: Yes, really. I'll call you tomorrow.

GERD: I hope you have a good meeting.

Timing: 10 minutes

Practice 3

This should be a brief exercise with the emphasis on diplomacy. Prepare students by eliciting a range of phrases that can be used to get off the phone – politely.

Transfer

Remind students of how they should combine their learning from this course with any work situations involving English.

Skills Checklist

Introduce discussion on the contents of the Skills Checklist by asking about the qualities of an effective telephone call. Suggest students think in terms of the headings *Voice, Structure* and *Style* and elicit ideas relating to these.

Under the heading *Structure*, students should suggest *Beginning, Middle* and *End*. Ask students to suggest what should be included under these three sub-headings.

Emphasise that the Skills Checklist offers only guidelines. Naturally in some situations there will be variations from these suggestions.

Note: This unit includes only passing reference to small talk. This aspect of communication is given more extensive treatment in Module 1, Socialising, Units 1 and 2.

Timing: 15 minutes

5 Unfortunately there's a problem ...

AIMS	■ Cross-cultural communication on the telephone (2)	■ Problem-solving on the telephone ■ Complaints

Briefing

This unit develops the cross-cultural theme introduced in Unit 4. The unit focuses on problem-solving, covering skills areas such as handling customer enquiries, complaining and dealing with complaints.

The Practice and Role play activities offer opportunities for handling problems from both sides, both telephoning about a difficulty and dealing with such a call. As with other telephone practice activities, have students sit in pairs, back-to-back. Even better, use internal phone links if they are available.

1:1 situation

The unit works well with a single student. You will need to take part in the role plays and adopt a more direct role in discussions, eliciting as much as you can but feeding in your own opinions where relevant.

In 1:1 classes you can also spend a little more time giving feedback on student performance, especially in the role plays.

Timing: 3 hours

1 Cross-cultural communication on the telephone (2)

1 The first exercise is a warmer, to focus students on good reading strategies. After just a few seconds, check the answers:

Key

  a) Communication across cultures, trying to reduce embarrassment.
  b) Five paragraphs.
  c) Therefore, probably five main ideas.

2 Before students read the text, remind them to look for the main points, not to try to understand everything. Remind them that a paragraph normally consists of a single topic and related comment.
Topic + comment → main idea = paragraph.
After five minutes, check the answers to the True / False exercise.

Key

  a) True
  b) True
  c) False
  d) False
  e) True
  f) False

3 Probably *e* (sensitivity, politeness). The text includes the phrase *Above all* ... Elicit any other comments or discussion on the text.

Timing: 15 minutes

2 Problem-solving on the telephone

◻◉ 1 Begin with a brief general discussion on what is meant by customer service. Ask what it involves, why it is important, etc. Then introduce the recording, explaining that a retailer, Lee Santana, calls Yoshinaga Takafumi, a representative of AKA Company, a Japanese telecommunications equipment supplier. On first listening a), ask students to identify the problem and the solution. On second listening b), ask them to identify aspects of customer service and c) to follow the structure of the call as shown in the Student's Book.

Key

a) Some telephone systems were despatched to agents but without operators' manuals. The suggested solution: Mr Santana will send a list of all his agents who have the telephone system and AKA will send manuals to all of them.

b) Yes. He is totally supportive of the customer. He immediately accepts responsibility and suggests a solution. He is apologetic and friendly.

c) Play the tape again, stopping it at relevant points, to show how it follows the given structure. Discuss the extent to which any problem-solving phone call will have this type of structure.

Refer to the style of the conversation. Relevant observations are: the people involved are clearly established partners but they use fairly normal style, family names preceded by Mr. Note that in the name Mr Yoshinaga Takafumi, the given name is Takafumi, the family name is Yoshinaga.

Tapescript

YOSHINAGA: Hello, Mr Santana. How are you today?

SANTANA: Very well, thank you.

YOSHINAGA: What can I do for you?

SANTANA: Well, unfortunately there's a problem with the order we received from you yesterday. It seems we haven't received the right quantity of manuals to support the HT telephone system. We sent the supplies to our sales reps, but several of them have called to say that there are no manuals enclosed.

YOSHINAGA: Oh dear. That's bad news. I am very sorry to hear that. And you don't know how many packages are without manuals?

SANTANA: No, because we haven't opened every pack. But in several of those that have been opened, there are none – no manuals.

YOSHINAGA: So … some of them have them. But … er … I'm very sorry about this inconvenience to you, Mr Santana. Listen, can I suggest the quickest solution – if it's okay with you? Of course, if you prefer a different solution we can do that, too, but let me suggest something.

SANTANA: Right, what do you suggest we do?

YOSHINAGA: Well, if you send us the address of *all* the sales reps you have distributed the phones to, we'll send out the manuals this afternoon by Fastair, entirely at our own cost and the manuals should arrive tomorrow or the next day at the latest.

SANTANA: All of them?

YOSHINAGA: Yes … it may be that some have them already, but we cannot be sure who – so the best thing is to send out a manual for every package.

SANTANA: Yes, yes, I see. That would be the best thing. OK, Mr Yoshinaga, I'll do that. I'll email you the list of all the agents we've sent the… the… er… packages to and leave it to you to resolve the problem of the manuals.

YOSHINAGA: Okay, thank you. And please accept our apologies for this delay, this … this mix-up. I assure you we'll do everything possible to find out why the mistake happened.

SANTANA: Fine, thanks for your quick action.

YOSHINAGA: Not at all. Thank you and goodbye for now. Do call if there is anything else.

SANTANA: Alright, thank you. Goodbye, Mr Yoshinaga.

YOSHINAGA: Goodbye.

Timing: 15 minutes

Language focus option

Write the given conversation structure on the board or on an OHP. Spend a few minutes eliciting alternative phrases for the various stages.

Practice 1

Introduce the situation: the Client Services Manager of Keene Investments telephones one of her staff, a financial adviser, with a problem.

Students should work in pairs, A and B. They may then switch roles and repeat the exercise to gain practice from both sides.

Give students four minutes to prepare and perform the conversation using the given prompts. After giving feedback, play the model version on the tape.

Tapescript

CHARLES: Hello, Charles Heppel speaking.

ERICA: Charles, it's Erica here. There's a problem, I'm afraid.

CHARLES: Oh yes, what's that?

ERICA: We've had a call from someone called Sandra Henson from London. She says she was expecting you yesterday but you didn't turn up. Do you know anything about it?

CHARLES: Hold on … Henson … yes. No … the appointment's for next week. She's got it wrong.

ERICA: Oh, I thought it would be something simple.

CHARLES: What did you say to her?

ERICA: Well, nothing really, only that you'd ring back.

CHARLES: Okay, I'll call her. I don't know why she got it wrong.

ERICA: You wrote to her, didn't you?

CHARLES: Yes, I even wrote. We agreed on the phone and then I wrote a letter as well …

ERICA: Oh well … sorry to trouble you.

CHARLES: No, not at all. I was just writing up the report on last month. Anyway, I'll call her and sort it out – and I'll be in the office in a day or two, so I'll see you then. Everything else okay?

ERICA: Oh yes, all's fine. A little quiet …

CHARLES: I see. Okay, bye for now.

ERICA: Bye then, Charles.

Timing: 15 minutes

3 Complaints

1 Introduce the dialogue. A dissatisfied customer, Hamid Nadimi of Ahmed Al-Hamid & Co. in Riyadh, calls a supplier of a pipeline system, Peter Carr, of Stella Communications plc, from England. After the first listening, students should answer a) what's the problem? Answer: There has been a delay in repairing valves in a pipe system.

b) Play the tape again if necessary, asking students to note the other information required by the incomplete flow chart:

Key

- The response: that Bains (the technician) needed to see what was required to repair the faults.
- Action decided: to contact Bains and say exactly what would happen.

Encourage discussion of Peter Carr's handling of the call. In fact, he does not immediately accept responsibility; he tries to make an excuse for his technician. On the other hand, he does not know the full facts and defends his colleague and his company.

Unfortunately, the customer is not happy. Peter should have apologised immediately and been more sympathetic. Remember the maxim 'The customer is always right', *even if he isn't*. Perhaps *before* Mr Bains went to Riyadh, his company should have accepted Al-Hamid's analysis, *or* explained why they would have to send the engineer to make a preliminary investigation. Further discussion on Peter Carr:

- he should have given a clear statement of action

- he should have apologised
- he should have made a commitment to ensure no repetition of the delay
- communication with the client should be better
- communication between Peter Carr and his engineer should be better
- perhaps Peter Carr and his engineer need training in customer service and communication skills.

Tapescript

RECEPTIONIST: Good morning. This is Stella Communications. How can I help you?

HAMID: Hello. My name's Hamid Nadimi from Ahmed Al-Hamid and Company in Riyadh. I'd like to speak to Peter Carr, please.

RECEPTIONIST: Could you hold for one moment, Mr Nadimi? Mr Carr's on another line – or shall I ask him to call you back?

HAMID: I'll hold.

RECEPTIONIST: Okay – I think he's free now ... you're through now, Mr Nadimi.

PETER: Hello, Mr Nadimi. How are things in Riyadh?

HAMID: Not as good as I had hoped, Mr Carr.

PETER: Oh, I'm sorry to hear that. What's wrong?

HAMID: You sent an engineer, a Mr Bains, to repair the faulty valves on the pipe system you installed last year and he came without the necessary equipment. He tells me it will take him a week to get what he needs. We told him what he needed and yet he came here with nothing.

PETER: I guess he had to make an inspection to see what he had to get to do the repair.

HAMID: Mr Carr. You know that is not true. We told you what was needed and now we have a further delay. It seems to me your engineer has wasted his time coming to Riyadh. And in the meantime, we cannot use the pipes.

PETER: Well, where is Mr Bains now, is he still with you?

HAMID: I think he has gone now. To his hotel. He told me he would return with the parts he needs but he didn't say when exactly.

PETER: Leave it with me, Mr Nadimi. I'll call him and talk to him myself. I'm sure we'll sort something out in a day or two.

HAMID: I hope so, Mr Carr, because you know, we are not very happy with the service you have provided for us. At the beginning it was fine, there were no problems, but now we have a little technical fault and we have wasted a lot of time.

PETER: I understand. Don't worry. We'll sort it out.

HAMID: Yes. It's very important, Mr Carr. We don't have much time.

PETER: Okay, I'll talk to Mr Bains and call you later today – or tomorrow morning.

HAMID: Right. I hope you have good news for me. Goodbye for now.

PETER: Goodbye, Mr Nadimi.

Timing: 20 minutes

2   Have students suggest a completely new version of the above problem, in which Peter Carr provides better customer service. They should work in pairs and roughly script what they say before reading their new versions.

Timing: 15 minutes

3 Homework or self-study task. Have students write the email to Mr Nadimi. Suggest that the email should reflect the best principles of customer service.

Here is a model answer.

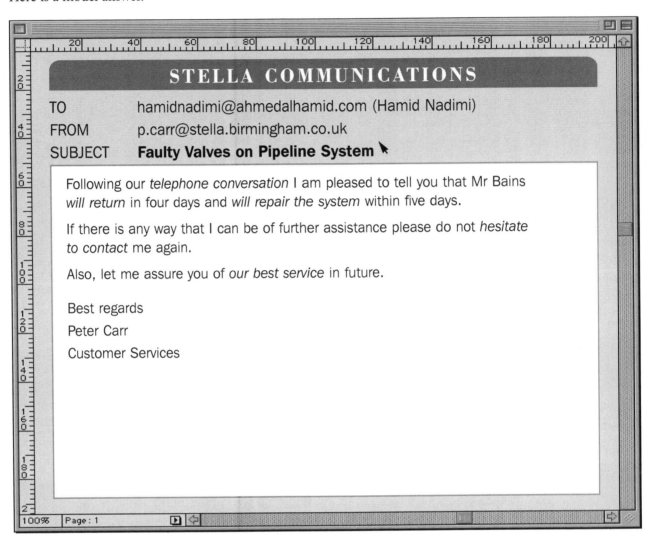

Timing: 10 minutes

Ask the students about what they understand by *within five days*. Note that the model is not perfect as the words *within five days* are not clear. Does this mean five days from the email or five days from his return?

Practice 2

Divide the class into As and Bs. The As should do the complaining. Then have As find different partners among the Bs and repeat the exercise,

this time with the Bs complaining. In this way everyone handles each situation twice, each time from a different perspective.

Tapescript

Extract 1

A: Now, it's about the printer I bought three months ago. It's broken down for a fourth time.

B: Oh dear. Well we'll get someone out to it.

A: Yes, but this time, can you please send them with a new printer? This one has been nothing but trouble.

B: Well, that may be the best solution. But really we should repair it.

A: Hmm. We've tried that. I think we want a completely new machine ...

Extract 2

A: It's the Royal City Hospital here, Pharmacy. We ordered 500 × 100ml of medicated gel – it hasn't arrived yet.

B: Er, I'm sorry about that. When did you place your order?

A: When? Three days ago.

B: Oh ... it should have arrived. Can you hold on, please, I'll check it.

Extract 3

A: Yes, it's Peter Redding here. I booked a flight to Lima, Iberia from Madrid. I leave tomorrow, but I haven't received my ticket yet. I've already phoned you about it twice.

B: Yes, in fact the courier took the ticket this morning, it should have arrived. It's possibly mixed up with a colleague's ticket, because we sent one at the same time to Manolo Gaspari. Is he a colleague of yours?

A: Yes, I know him. But it shouldn't have gone to him. It should have been addressed to me.

B: I'm very sorry, but if you contact him, he ought to have it. If not, please call me back.

PHOTOCOPIABLE © Cambridge University Press 2003

Timing: 30 minutes

Language focus option

Spend extra time on some of the recordings, focusing on key language of complaints and handling complaints. Have students identify and repeat key phrases. Some students may wish to write some examples down.

Do not spend too long on this – use it only to support students for whom this language presents particular difficulties.

Practice 3

Have students work in pairs to improvise a conversation based on the flow chart. Give support and feedback where required. Then play the model answer on the tape.

Tapescript

TAO LOON: Hello, Sales Office here.

LUISA: Hello, my name's Luisa Dominguez. I'm ringing from Spain – from Berraondo Company.

TAO LOON: How can I help you, Ms Dominguez?

LUISA: The problem concerns a printer order. Let me give you the order number... it's HF5618. It's... it's for 20 printers. The problem is that only 17 have arrived.

TAO LOON: Really? I am surprised to hear that.

LUISA: Well, I'm afraid it's the second time we've received an incomplete delivery and nobody told us there would only be 17.

TAO LOON: Well, no, I think it was probably an administration mistake.

LUISA: Yes, I'm sure. Now, we need the other three printers urgently. Delays are causing us problems with our customers. They are rather unhappy.

TAO LOON: Okay, er, at the moment we have some stock problems.

LUISA: Well, can you give me a delivery date – it's very urgent.

TAO LOON: Right... let me see. We can promise you a despatch next Monday.

LUISA: No, I'm sorry, that's not good enough. We need despatch now.

TAO LOON: I am very sorry... that's not possible. But we'll despatch on Monday, I assure you.

LUISA: Well, will you please send an email to confirm that?

TAO LOON: Of course. And I do apologise for the problem.

LUISA: Right, goodbye for now.

TAO LOON: Goodbye.

PHOTOCOPIABLE © Cambridge University Press 2003

Timing: 10 minutes

Role play

Where appropriate refer students to the Language Checklist as part of the preparation for the role play.

Timing: 20 minutes

Transfer 1

This is a general discussion on problems and complaints in students' working environment – or their personal lives. Try to elicit examples of problem-solving on the telephone. Find out if such problem-solving on the phone involves colleagues or clients, or third parties (banks, offices, services, etc.).

Transfer 2

This can lead to a role play based on students' real-life situations. They should work in pairs to prepare two conversations typical of the sorts of problems or complaints they are individually faced with at work. Each individual should think of a situation relevant to himself / herself, then explain the roles involved to his / her partner, then perform the conversation. See Unit 3 for a fuller explanation.

6 Planning and getting started

Briefing

The module begins with some fairly extensive work on presentation technique. An effective route into developing presentation skills is to discuss the qualities of good preparation and presentation technique. The unit establishes some key principles concerning preparation and the audience before progressing to the vital area of giving a good introduction. Students produce their own introductions after considering two examples. Later units look at use of visuals, the main body of the presentation and the end, including handling questions and discussion.

As in other units, encourage students to reach their own conclusions and to contribute their ideas. Your role is to support and guide learners through the material, channelling their responses.

Some students who are actually in work may approach the module with a particular presentation in mind. In other words they anticipate giving a talk fairly soon. it is quite possible – and indeed desirable – to combine preparation for such a talk with the four units in this module, each dealing with a discrete part of the overall task of giving presentations. The units are designed to allow students to work on a major presentation, on a topic of their choice, throughout the module. However, this is not obligatory.

Language focus

Although there is a high profile given to target language in this unit – and in the next one – further exploitation can be based on the tapescript. You may choose to draw attention to aspects of pronunciation as illustrated in the recordings of introductions.

1:1 situation

The unit works well with one student. You will probably need to be even more supportive in eliciting the ideas, commenting on them and contributing your own. You will also need to play the role of audience in practice tasks.

Timing: 3 hours

1 Presentation technique and preparation

1   Ask students to look at the introductory picture on page 55.
    Elicit ideas on presentation technique which can be drawn from the picture.
    Have students write 'What makes a good presentation?' on a piece of paper. In pairs, get them to write notes for two or three minutes. Prompt them to think about content, appearance and style.

Note: Even students with little experience of giving presentations will have ideas, especially as almost everyone has seen presentations, good or bad, in various contexts, if only on television or at school!

Then get pairs to double up, compare notes and discuss.

After two or three more minutes, ask for ideas from each group. Write suggestions on the board. Do this semi-systematically, grouping related ideas under key words like *Organisation, Visual support,*

Voice, Content, Physical aspects (appearance, gesture, eye contact, etc.). You may paraphrase what students say but keep to their ideas.

Refer to the Skills Checklist, which can serve as a permanent reminder of key considerations to ensure that a presentation is a good one.

2   Tell your students that the text is from a US management training textbook. An experienced presenter writes about presentation technique. Students do not have to read the text in detail or spend a long time on it. The main task should not take more than ten minutes.

Warn the class not to read the text in detail or use a dictionary while they read it for the first time. *Their sole objective should be to match the paragraphs a–g to the correct point 1–7.*

Then you may spend five minutes dealing with any questions on vocabulary.

Finally, spend an additional five minutes for the discussion on which point is the most important. Different students can say which advice they think is the most important *for them.*

Key

1   Choose visuals to support the presentation. (c)
2   Have a simple, clear structure.   (a)
3   Show enthusiasm.   (g)
4   Use PowerPoint.   (d)
5   Making informal presentations.   (e)
6   Consider the audience.   (b)
7   Dealing with nerves.   (f)

Time: 30 minutes

3   Spend a maximum of five minutes on this, first in pairs, then elicit ideas from the class. The tapescript for question 4 which follows is quite comprehensive, so do not add much to students' suggestions. Write them on the board.

4   Introduce the recording. Check that students understand the icons. Elicit the eight key areas in preparing a presentation. Do the activity and check that learners number the pictures in the right order.

Key

1E: audience, 2B: objectives, 3A: structure, 4H: visuals, 5F: writing out some or all of the presentation, 6D: practice, 7G: checking the language, 8C: the room and the equipment.

Tapescript

GEORGE: Right, now let's think about the preparation of the presentation. What has to be … what do you have to do to prepare it?

SARA: The most important thing is to know about the audience, find out about them

LUIGI: Yes, but you need to make sure about your objectives first, so decide on the objectives – what you want the talk to achieve.

SARA: Yes, but to do that you need to know about the audience – their knowledge, what they want to know, you know everything like that.

LUIGI: Yes, all that's important …

HAL: Yes, true …

GEORGE: So, audience and objectives.

OTHERS: Yes / Right / Okay.

HAL: And the third thing you have to sort out is content, collect information, organise it, decide on a structure.

SARA: Yes, get a good structure, I agree … Then once the structure is okay, well, you need visuals, any graphs, you know, that sort of thing …

GEORGE: Yes, the visual supports.

SARA: Then, well, you *could* write it all out. At least the introduction – just to practise it. Some people write out everything, some don't. It depends.

GEORGE: Yes, I think that's a good point. But practice is really very important. A key … key part of the preparation is to actually practise it, to give the presentation – practise … until you could do it just from notes. Then well … what else?

LUIGI: Check all the language, keep it simple, make sure there're no mistakes on the visuals. Spelling and all that.

HAL: And I think you should check that the room is okay, check the equipment is okay. And maybe also… PowerPoint, you know. If you use PowerPoint, make sure your computer and the disk, or the data projector, make sure it all works.

GEORGE: Yes, PowerPoint, of course.

SARA: If you don't know PowerPoint, go on a course. Learn it.

GEORGE: Yes, using presentations software can help enormously.

Timing: 20 minutes

Discussion

Elicit students' own views on what they have heard and see if they have any personal preferences concerning preparation for and practice of presentations. There is no one way and the best presenters probably have a different approach depending on the topic, the audience, etc.

Refer again to the Skills Checklist.

Timing: 5 minutes

2 The audience

Briefly discuss the proposition that the audience is the most important consideration in preparing a presentation. Ask why the audience is so important: a speaker needs to hold the audience's attention – or the talk is a failure.

1 Introduce the task. Ask students to suggest what caused the problems. Possible explanations:

Key
a) Technical level of talk is too high / Speaker is saying something completely wrong or incomprehensible.
b) The talk is boring, too long, or delivered monotonously, no changes in pace, volume, tone, etc.
c) The visual is too small or too detailed.
d) The speaker is talking too quietly.
e) The structure of the talk was not clear.

Additional notes:
- Dress appropriately – many cultures are very conservative in dress.
- Some cultures may be offended by jokes or not understand them. Remember, humour does not always travel well.
- Avoid references to topics that are taboo in a society – once again, know the audience and their expectations.

Option

If you think it appropriate, elicit examples of the characteristics of an audience that would affect the type of presentation. Possible features are: technical level, interests, experience, age, responsibilities, ability to concentrate, required knowledge, expectations, ability to remember, size of audience, etc.

2 In pairs students should select two of the given situations and discuss answers to the questions a–f for each one.

Then individually students decide on another situation – relating to their own experience, not the situations given in the book – and provide answers to the same questions a–f, which they discuss with their partner.

Then briefly, with the whole class, elicit short answers to a–f for each of the four given situations and ask volunteers for comments on their own choices.

Option

Make own situation a self-study or homework task.

Key
Tokyo medical congress
a) Probably very formal.
b) High expectations in terms of technical support, a fair amount of detail and clearly a lot of expertise.
c) High level of specialist knowledge – audience are experts.
d) Depends on congress organisation – probably less than an hour.

e) Depends on congress organisation – probably questions follow.

f) Use of visual supports with key information, plus later publication of Congress Proceedings.

Purchasing and Product Managers of a Taiwanese company

a) Probably semi-formal.

b) High expectations in terms of technical support, a fair amount of detail and clearly a lot of expertise.

c) High level of specialist knowledge – at least the Product Manager will be very expert, the Purchasing Manager perhaps less so.

d) Depends on objectives and on complexity of equipment. Could be a very long presentation, even a whole day – or a one-hour presentation might be enough.

e) Probably interruptions are encouraged to make everything clear as the presenter goes along.

f) Use of visual supports, photographs, diagrams, or the actual machine itself. Follow-up documentation will also be available.

Internal meeting / Administrative staff

a) Informal.

b) Reasonably high expectations in terms of speaker's knowledge.

c) The audience will probably have good background knowledge but have come to learn about a new system.

d) Probably short – thought it might be half a day!

e) Interruptions encouraged.

f) Probably illustrations, possibly handouts.

A staff meeting / Charity event

a) Informal.

b) Low expectations.

c) The audience have come to hear ideas.

d) Probably short – five or ten minutes?

e) Interruptions encouraged.

f) Keep to clear simple structure making one or two important points.

Timing: 30 minutes

3 Structure (1) The introduction

Refer to students' ideas on 'What makes a good presentation' from page 55. Highlight structure and explain that you are going to look at this in more detail. Ask students what they understand by structure or organisation. Elicit, if you can, the idea of a beginning, a middle and an end.

Explain that you are going to focus on the beginning, because in any presentation it is crucial.

1 Before looking at page 59, ask students to suggest what should be included in an introduction to a formal / semi-formal presentation. Write suggestions on the board.
  Introduce the task, check understanding of the scale. Elicit answers. A possible answer is:

Key

Subject / Title of talk.	1
Introduction to oneself, job, title, etc.	4
Reference to questions and / or discussion.	2
Reference to the programme for the day.	4
Reference to how long you are going to speak for.	3
Reference to using PowerPoint.	5
The scope of your talk: what is and is not included.	4
An outline of the structure of your talk.	1
A summary of the conclusions.	4

Discuss points arising. Another possible inclusion is 'Background', though this could be the first part of the main body of the presentation.

Note: There are no hard rules about what should be included. Most suggestions here are open to discussion and variation, depending on circumstances.

2 Introduce the first example as the beginning of a presentation on marketing plans for a new Telco telecommunications system. Play it once and check these answers:

Key

a) No.

b) No clear structure – seems to be talking about brand identity – no mention of marketing plans. A totally unfocused introduction.

c) Impossible to identify structure.

Note: This introduction is very difficult to understand – probably also difficult for native speakers of English. It is important that learners know *why*: it is because of the answers to the above questions.

Tapescript

SPEAKER: Thank you for coming today. As you know, I want to talk about the marketing plans. Brand identity is a key issue and what it means is how we are seen by our customers and how our products are recognised and what our consumers think of us as a company. And I should also say, what they think of our products and the name … what Telco means for them. And advertising is part of it of course, though not something I am going to talk about now except to say that as for brand image, it's important in that area too, advertising that is.

Reiterate the point about how crucial it is to give information on the structure of the talk. This helps the audience to follow the talk and clearly states what will be included.

3 Introduce the second example of an introduction – it is about design plans for a new production plant in Taipei, Taiwan. Play the extract once only. Check students' answers to questions a–c.

Key

a) Very good.
b) Clear and structured.

c)
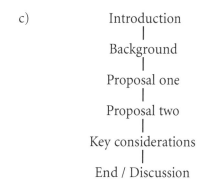

Tapescript

SPEAKER: Okay, thanks. I'm here to talk about the design proposals for the production plant at Taipei. My talk will be in three parts followed by a 30-minute discussion. I'm going to start with the background to each proposal – something about our negotiations with the Taiwanese government – then in the second part I'll go over the main characteristics of each proposal, Proposal One and Proposal Two. Then in the third part I'll highlight some key considerations we have to bear in mind. Finally, I'll end with an invitation to ask questions or make any comments you like. We'll discuss matters arising from the talk … Okay? So to begin with, a few words on the history.

Language focus option

You may wish to spend some time focusing on the key structural language in this extract. Highlight the phrases used to describe structure, to say what each part will be about. Note the use of *will, going to* and the contracted form *I'll*.

In any case, the next three exercises have a clear language focus.

4 A quick oral exercise, optionally a self-study or homework follow-up. Ask students to suggest possible phrases. Remind them that there are various options, so individuals may suggest different answers.

Check suggestions for each prompt. Play the model version at an appropriate moment. Point out how this combines all the phrases into a single introduction.

Tapescript

SPEAKER: a) Good afternoon everyone. b) My name's Arnold Layton. I'm a (geophysicist) for (Elf Aquitaine), with special responsibility for (analysing new fields in the North Sea). c) I'm going to talk about (some recent research into new methods of detecting oil in shallow waters). d) I've divided my talk into three parts. First, (research that we have done). Then (I'll report on some published research from other companies), and finally (I'll talk about what this may mean for our exploration activities). e) Please interrupt if at any time you have any questions or something is not clear. f) My talk will last about (half an hour). g) Later my colleague Jacques Flambert will be showing a video on …

Be prepared to focus on the language used in this model example if students need further guidance or clarification.

Timing: 45 minutes

Practice 1

This guided task is optional. Some students may prefer to go straight to Practice 2, where they can choose the topic and no structure guidance is given. In this case, just play the model answer.

Timing: 10 minutes

Tapescript

SPEAKER: Right, I want to say something about the new safety conditions for production staff. My talk will be in three parts. First, I'll tell you about the new protective clothing. Then I'll explain about the training in accident prevention, and the final part of my talk explains changes to working practices. After my talk I'll be happy to answer any questions and we can have a discussion about these new proposals.

Practice 2

The aim again is for students to produce language which echoes the second introduction on the tape. Give students two minutes to prepare a 30–60-second introduction. Refer to the Language Checklist.

Stress that students may choose any topic they like – the objective is that they explain the subject and the structure accurately and clearly. It should be a one-minute *introduction only*.

Hear individuals' introductions. Give feedback on structure and language.

Timing: 15 minutes

Transfer

This is designed to cover virtually any student's situation. It can be based on a company well known to the student – not necessarily his / her place of work – or on a school, college, sports club, etc.

Preparation

Possibly as homework: ask students to prepare a *one or two-minute introduction* to a talk. Remind them to look at the Skills Checklist, to make notes but preferably *not* write the text. Weaker, less confident students may need to. Suggest practice at home.

Performance

Students can give their introductions in class, standing up, using notes only. Some may begin the habit of using cue cards.

Planning and practising a presentation throughout the module

Either students can begin preparation for an actual presentation they have to make in the future, with the Transfer exercises throughout the module all used in preparation for this.

Or students may use the Transfer tasks

throughout the module to create a single presentation on a subject of their choice, either business or study-related, or concerned with world affairs, the environment, politics or economics, etc.

Developing self-assessment skills

Record introductions. Get students to comment on their own performance. Self-assessment is an important learning strategy. Recordings should help develop the habit of constructive self-criticism and awareness of how to improve. This also helps students to see progress and to recognise good performance.

Feedback

Your role is to guide, point out things they miss, and above all to encourage and praise good performance. In a group with good personal dynamics, encourage constructive criticism. But beware potential sensitivities, especially where there are different status levels in a group. Do not press individuals to be critical of others if you detect any problems.

Take care not to spend too long on individuals in a group class. Time management has to be strict and fair. As this unit deals only with introductions, each student's contributions are likely to be very short. Do not be afraid to move on, suggesting that students look at their recordings in more detail later. Record students consecutively so they can do this, not one on top of another with feedback after each one.

Option

Repeat the exercise with the same or a different topic.

Skills Checklist

As in other units the Skills Checklist should be introduced as a focus for discussion. If you can, copy it onto a transparency and show it on a screen. Point out that the Skills Checklist is a more complete version of students' response to the question *What are the characteristics of a good presentation?* The main difference is that it focuses on *Planning and Preparation.* Under this heading are nine key areas: audience, competence, content, structure, delivery, visual aids, practice, room and language. Go through each of these, providing extra explanation where necessary. Get learners to explain what they understand by the points made in each section.

Stress the importance of good preparation. Even informal presentations delivered by experts require preparation.

Do not feel that you have to explain everything on this page. Elicit students' ideas as much as you can. Most adults, even those with little experience of actually giving presentations, will have ideas on this. Some points may need special clarification:

a) Under the heading 'competence' can be found 'knowledge'. This means everything the presenter knows about the subject. It is assumed that someone giving a presentation knows about the subject and has special expertise. If not, he / she should be doing something else!

b) 'Presentation technique' covers everything studied in this unit (and the next three).

c) Under 'Content' appears 'number of key ideas'. This means not overloading the audience.

Note: Unit 7 has more on using visual supports.

Timing: 15 minutes

7 Image, impact and making an impression

AIMS	■ Using visual aids: general principles	■ Describing change
	■ Talking about the content of visual aids	

Briefing

This unit looks at using visual supports within the context of presentations. However, many of the principles discussed are equally relevant to using visual aids in meetings and negotiations.

After an overview of some general principles on using visual aids, the unit focuses on key language, including a check on terms used for describing change. There are plenty of opportunities to hear target language before using it in different practice exercises. For additional student support, refer also to the Language Checklist.

Practice activities encourage students to find and present pictures from various sources and also to design their own.

Of course you can encourage your students to use PowerPoint and other computer aids for giving presentations. While these certainly help with the visual aspect of presenting, students still need help with the language to describe visuals, whether using PowerPoint, or computer-produced acetates on an OHT, or a flipchart.

Video recording

This unit is especially suitable for video recording the short practice tasks. Do not spend too long on them. Students should first comment on their own performance, but also encourage constructive observations about each other's efforts.

The video camera creates useful pressure in the training situation. Remember, such pressure is nothing compared to real commercial and reputation pressures.

1:1 situation

The unit works well with 1:1 classes and is especially suited to individuals with specific presentation needs. As usual, you may need to be more actively involved in eliciting information, discussing texts and ideas, taking roles and playing the audience.

Timing: approximately 2.5 hours

1 Using visual aids: general principles

1 Use the opening cartoons to stimulate discussion, eliciting students' comments. Even students with little experience of giving presentations will have seen others using visual aids, so most people should contribute.

The first cartoon makes the point that a good visual can make a point more effectively than a long speech, the second is vitally important as many non-native speakers (as well as many first language users) rely too heavily on gadgetry.

Presenters using PowerPoint should be absolutely sure the computer and data projector link is set up correctly in advance.

2 This is a brief check exercise. Learners used to a business context will know several of these items. Answers are given here:

Key

OHP

Screen

Computer /
PowerPoint

Slide projector

OHTs / Transparencies

Slides

Flipchart

Whiteboard

3   This set of pictures is more challenging. They illustrate common failings in technique. Elicit students' interpretations and comments on what is happening in each picture, where a variety of bad practices are shown.

Then elicit possible recommendations – you may suggest others. Here are some suggestions based on the pictures:
- Write clearly (print).
- Position screen where everyone can see it – in a corner often works best – and do not stand in front of the machine obscuring the image.
- Do not use detailed numerical information or too much detail.
- Do not turn your back on the audience.
- Choose your media carefully. If you use a monitor, make sure it is big enough for the room and audience.

4   Students should not spend long reading the text – three minutes should be ample to identify the information asked for. Encourage them to use highlighter pens rather than write out answers.

Key

a)
- Visuals make information more memorable.
- Help the speaker.

- Show information which is not easily expressed in words.
- Highlight information.
- Cause audience to employ another sense to receive information.
- Bring variety and therefore increase audience's attention.
- Save time.
- Clarify complex information.

b)
- presenters sometimes place the major emphasis on visual aids and relegate themselves to the minor role of narrator or technician
- visuals must support what the speaker says
- it is not enough just to read what the visual says.

Timing: 20 minutes

2 Talking about the content of visual aids

This section provides students with broad exposure to descriptions of a wide variety of visual supports, introducing the target vocabulary in a meaningful context. The recordings provide models for the kind of language used to describe visual supports. Students will have the opportunity to use this language later. To begin with, understanding it and seeing how it combines with visual images is the first concern.

1   The exercise is to check what students already know: many may know some of the answers. They may get the right answers by carefully using a process of elimination. Have students work in pairs then go through the answers. If there are mistakes, come back to the task later in the lesson and in the future by using quick sketches on the board and asking students what they show.

Key

a) diagram	b) bar graph (histogram)
c) line graph	d) picture
e) table	f) pie chart
g) flow chart	h) plan
i) map	

Discuss the above. Draw attention to *rows* and *columns* in a table and *segments* in a pie chart. Ask learners to find other examples in other books, reports or magazines.

Go on to the next section with the first graph:

j)　solid line　　　k)　dotted line

l)　broken line

Discuss these, check understanding. Go on to the next graph:

m)　vertical axis　　n)　horizontal axis

o)　curve　　　　　p)　fluctuating line

q)　undulating line

Discuss these as necessary. In all cases, check in a subsequent lesson by bringing examples or by drawing quick sketches to ask students what the items are called.

2　a) Introduce the recording, which contains four short extracts from one presentation. Ask students to match each extract to the correct diagram a–d.

Key

1 = C,　2 = A,　3 = B,　4 = D.

Tapescript

Extract 1

SPEAKER: My talk concentrates on the Kildale Gap location and the planning we have carried out so far. It's divided into three *main* parts – as you can see – this short introduction, then first, a few words on the site at Kildale Gap, then an overview of the environmental costs. After the environmental costs, we'll look at other costs. After that, we'll break for a discussion. If everyone is happy with that …

Extract 2

SPEAKER: Now … the first picture to show you on this, on the environmental costs, clearly shows that construction accounts for over 60%, while the environmental costs amount to around 12%, shown by this segment here. That's a lot less than the land purchase …

Extract 3

SPEAKER: Moving on … I thought you would be interested in a comparison – looking at the costs of the environmental expenditure for Kildale Gap – with some other possible sites – and as you can see by the chart – it's very good. In fact, it would cost well below the average. Only one is a slight bit … small bit cheaper …

Extract 4

SPEAKER: This picture, the next one here, shows initial investment, rising in the first year, beginning to fall during year two, then – you see – falling after about a year and a half … then the decline in investment costs will continue …

b) Play the recording again. Ask students to identify a key point from each extract (they can use the relevant diagram to help them).

Key

Extract 1: The talk has three main parts before the discussion.

Extract 2: 12% of costs are environmental (60% construction. Land purchase a lot more than environmental costs).

Extract 3: The site has lower than average environmental costs.

Extract 4: Investment will fall after eighteen months.

Language focus option

If you like, play the recording a third time, asking students to concentrate on language used to introduce and describe the pictures. Some key phrases, typical of describing such pictures, can be identified. Focus in particular on:

… It's divided into three *main* parts – as you can see …

… Now … the first picture to show you on this, … , clearly shows that … while … … shown by this segment here.

… Moving on … I thought you would be interested in a comparison – looking at the … … as you can see by the chart …
This picture, the next one here, shows … … then … you see …

3 Introduce the next visuals from a presentation on the environment.
a) Get pairs of students to work together and suggest a typical structure to describe the graph. Hear some suggestions.
b) Play the recording to accompany the graph, and ask students to compare the version on the tape with their own and to identify the speaker's main point: that carbon dioxide emissions have gone up – and are still going up – very dramatically.

Then elicit or point out this typical structure in the description:

Introduction
What the graph is about
|
Explanation
What the two axes represent
|
Message
Highlight key information

Respond to any questions or comments.
c) Play the extract again and have students fill in the missing words.

Tapescript

SPEAKER: Now I'd like to show you this graph. It shows the rate of increase in CO_2 emissions between 1950 and 1990. On the left-hand vertical axis you see the CO_2 emissions in millions of tonnes, while the horizontal axis shows time over forty years. The three lines show… the global total at the top, the broken line here is OECD countries, or developed countries. The dotted line shows non-OECD, or developing countries.

What we can see here is, quite clearly, a sharp increase in CO_2 emissions. This increase is global, look at the top line here, but the graph shows that it's strongest in developing countries. In OECD countries, the rate of increase is slower. Up to 2000, the situation continued just the same …

Key

1 Now I'd like a) **to show you** this graph. It b) **shows** the c) **rate of increase** in CO_2 emissions between 1950 and 1990.
2 On d) **the left-hand vertical axis** you see the CO_2 emissions in millions of tons, while the e) **horizontal axis shows** time over forty years. f) **The three lines show** the global total at the top, the broken line here is OECD countries, or developed countries. The dotted line shows non-OECD, or developing countries.
3 What we g) **can see** here is, quite clearly, h) **a sharp increase** in CO_2 emissions …

4 Introduce the next two visual aids from the same presentation. This is a controlled practice exercise, with students working in pairs. If they are short of language, direct them to the Language Checklist or offer other help as necessary. Prompt students towards a good description of each picture.
● Remind students to think about the *structure* of their description.
● Remind them to choose just two or three *main points* to emphasise from each picture.
● Allow two or three minutes' preparation.
● Get individuals to volunteer explanations of one or both pictures.
Finally, play the recording. Ask students to compare their versions with the recording. Check understanding of the language used, especially terms like *segment, row, column*.

Tapescript

SPEAKER: Now, the … my next picture here … a pie chart … shows the current sources for energy production. The main thing to notice is that oil, coal and gas are the main sources. Look here, mostly oil, then coal at 23% and natural gas almost as much. So 25% comes from other sources and a tiny 0.1% from renewable sources, geothermal, wind or solar energy … Now let's look at the table here. This shows some comparisons between selected EU states on electricity generation. The striking thing here is the French dependency on nuclear power, 76%. Then look at Sweden, also with quite a high proportion of electricity coming from nuclear power, but 50% coming from renewable sources, in this column here. The EU average shows quite a spread, but the UK, for example, has only 4% of its electricity coming from renewable sources. That's much lower than the EU average. The UK of course has a lot of oil and gas reserves, while France and Sweden, for example, do not.

PHOTOCOPIABLE   © Cambridge University Press 2003

Timing: 45 minutes

Language focus option

Spend some more time focusing on the language used in this recording, referring to the Language Checklist at the same time. Hear more examples of students' attempts to describe the two pictures in their books.

Practice 1

There now follow several more practice tasks based on the environmental theme. Help students as much as is necessary, perhaps running the first as a class task, before having individuals work alone or in pairs.

Key

a) Now *let me show you this graph, the Fossil Fuel Farewell graph, from a study originally from Greenpeace.*
b) It shows *how over the next 100 years renewable energy could supply all the world's energy needs.*

c) The vertical *axis* shows *energy in Exajoules,* while *the horizontal axis shows decades up 2100.*
d) Clearly we can see that *oil, coal and natural gas, and nuclear energy, is gradually replaced by biomass and solar and wind-generated energy.*

Tapescript

SPEAKER: Now let me show you this graph, the Fossil Fuel Farewell graph, from a study originally from Greenpeace. It shows how over the next 100 years renewable energy could supply all the world's energy needs. The vertical axis shows energy in exajoules, while the horizontal axis shows decades up to 2100. Clearly we can see that oil, coal and natural gas, and nuclear energy, are gradually replaced by biomass and solar and wind-generated energy. In other words, all energy is provided, or could be provided, by renewable energy sources. The graph also suggests an end to the use of nuclear power by about 2012.

PHOTOCOPIABLE   © Cambridge University Press 2003

Further practice options: Air pollution and the environment

Use the photocopiable material on page 57 for further practice.

- Suggest five or six minutes to prepare a brief description of all three.
- Suggest working individually, in pairs or in threes.
- Refer to the Language Checklist on page 73 of the Student's Book.
- Remind students to be selective, to highlight only key points from each one.
- Different students might choose different points to highlight.
- Select groups or individuals to present part or all of their descriptions.

Note 1: Weaker students may prefer to write down what they are going to say. In all but the weakest cases, try to discourage this. It would be more natural, and would help students' confidence if they manage the task using only the pictures themselves as support.

Note 2: The table is very detailed. In a stand-up presentation it would probably be inappropriate (see earlier in the unit). It could however be a useful type of visual where handouts are used, as in a round-table meeting.

Tip: A suggestion for presentation purposes is to have the pictures blown up and put on an overhead transparency.

Tapescript

SPEAKER: The first picture shows the relative contribution to the greenhouse effect of various gases. The most significant is CO_2, with over half. Another important greenhouse gas is methane, accounting for 15%. But the combined total for all the CFCs is 24%.

Now let's look at another graph, showing changing world temperatures between 1990 and 2100. The graph shows a minimum and a maximum effect, with a range between about 1.3° and 4° Celsius. The line here shows the observable rise in global warming, which is not regular, but the trend is clearly an increase. The implications are, of course, important.

Now we come on to a table showing the rate of deforestation in various countries. In many countries, deforestation is a serious issue. Just to take a couple of key points from the table. The rate of loss in Brazil – the country with the largest amount of forest – is enormous – up to 50,000 square kilometres a year. In Nigeria the amount is quite small, but what's striking about Nigeria is the enormous percentage of forest lost each year: 14.3% in a year … clearly the situation is perilous.

Timing: 30 minutes

3 Describing change

1 This section is to check what students already know. It could be given for homework or self-study. Undoubtedly some students will also learn new words or better understand words that are presently only part of their passive knowledge.

Key

    c) climbed slightly
    d) declined a little
    e) increased steadily
    f) dropped markedly
    g) rose dramatically

Note: The phrases above show verb + modifier combinations. Point out that the same meaning can be produced by using adjective + noun combinations, e.g. increased steadily → a steady increase.

2 Encourage use of a dictionary, especially to find out equivalent nouns or verbs. Explain that not all the verbs that can be used here have a noun form, e.g. *to go up*.

The key given here provides some possible answers. There may be others, or they may be in a different order, etc. Check the paradigms of irregular verbs, e.g. rise, rose, risen; fall, fell, fallen.

Key

    a) to go up
        to rise / a rise
        to climb / a climb
        to grow / a growth
    b) to go down
        to fall / a fall
        to decline / a decline
        to drop / a drop
    c) to level off / out
        to remain steady
    d) to reach a peak
        to peak
    e) to improve / an improvement
        to get better
    f) to get worse / a downturn

Timing: 20 minutes

Role play

Suggest students refer to the Language Checklist in preparing for the role play and the subsequent practice tasks.

Check that students understand the mechanics of the task. Explain that the objective is to give a fluent and complete explanation of the picture, beginning by giving the title and then explaining the picture in detail. First Student A explains the picture on File card 12A, giving plenty of detail. However if Student A misses anything or information is not forthcoming, Student B should ask questions.

Your aim is that the students should transfer the information satisfactorily. It is probably best not to record students this time but note any major problems and offer prompts where necessary. You may wish to spend a little time clearing up any doubts or difficulties over language after the task has been completed. Then reverse roles, B describing File card 12B.

Tip: File card visual supports can be enlarged on a photocopier and transferred onto an overhead transparency for better effect. This can be done with any good picture.

Timing: 10 minutes

Practice 2

Have students draw a line graph, then give a brief explanation of what it shows. They can invent the information on the graph if they wish.
Preparation should take only a couple of minutes, presentation one minute.

They should not need to write anything except as part of the actual visual support. For weaker students, offer encouragement and praise: some learners may be doubly intimidated by having to stand up and present, and having to describe a graph.

Timing: 15 minutes

Further practice option

A possible homework option is to ask students to find a visual in a newspaper, magazine or other published source and to prepare to give a description (lasting no more than two minutes) in class. Remind them to note the way the visual is described or referred to in the article. Students may also choose to use materials relating to work or studies.

Then ask them to imagine they have to present the information described in the picture to a meeting of interested people. They should prepare a short description for presentation in class. It would help if you can transfer the picture to an OHT.

Transfer

Ask students to think of their own professional or study situation and to prepare any pictures or visuals for use in a presentation. They should prepare what to say about each one.

Use a video recorder if one is available.

If you have no video the feedback will inevitably require you to make notes while the presentation is being made or immediately afterwards.

Encourage students to be self-critical, to notice their weaknesses and to suggest improvements. Remember that video without sound is also a useful way to review how visual aids are presented. Check students' performance in terms of the points mentioned below:

Video with sound off
- the appearance and design of the visual
- body position in relation to 'the audience'
- any gestures, use of hands, etc.
- maintaining eye contact

Video recording or audio recording
- the clarity of message
- the appropriacy of the words used
- highlighting of the main facts
- the amount of detail – not too much
- correct level of formality

Option: Project work

If your class consists of students who are not yet in work, remember that a very useful activity to accompany their studying English – and their use of this book – would be to engage them on a project (on a topic agreed between you and the students) where they have to find out information, compile it in some kind of written form (for example notes and visual supports, graphics, etc.) and present it to you and other students. They could do this individually or in pairs, or in small groups. This unit and this Transfer activity provide an ideal opportunity to practise part of the presentation phase of such a project.

Air pollution and the environment

Look at the three pictures below, all from the same presentation on 'Air pollution and the environment'. Prepare a brief description, saying what each picture represents and identifying key points from each one.

You may choose to use some of the language you have already heard. Also, look at the Language Checklist on page 73 in the Student's Book.

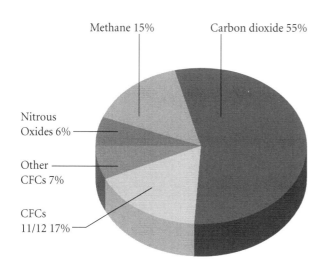

Fig. 1. Gases contributing to greenhouse effect.

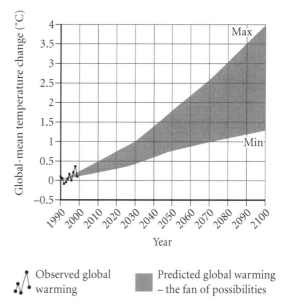

Fig. 2. Changing world temperatures

Country deforestation (plus area) in sq. miles.	Original forest cover	Present forest cover	Deforestation per year (plus %)
Bolivia (1.1 m)	95,000	75,000	1,500 (2.1)
Brazil (8.5 m)	2,850,000	2,000,000	50,000 (2.3)
India (3.3 m)	1,600,000	165,000	4,000 (2.4)
Mexico (2.0 m)	400,000	170,000	7,000 (4.2)
Nigeria (0.9 m)	70,000	25,000	10,000 (14.3)
Thailand (0.5 m)	420,000	74,000	6,000 (8.4)
Zaire (2.3 m)	1,250,000	1,000,000	4,000 (0.4)

Fig. 3. Deforestation rates.

8 The middle of the presentation

AIMS	■ Holding the audience's attention	■ Linking ideas
	■ Structure (2) The main body	■ Sequencing
	■ Listing information	

Briefing

The focus of this unit is on how to use language to make the presentation both easier to understand and more memorable. The context used is the main body of the presentation, where there is the greatest danger of a rambling and incoherent style.

Language focus

The recorded extracts include clear examples of the key areas of language in this unit. They offer the opportunity for more detailed study of the language where desired. See also the Language Checklist.

1:1 situation

You may record students' efforts in the Practice tasks, which might make feedback easier, especially in terms of eliciting student self-assessment. One-to-one students may benefit from more detailed analysis, but take care not to labour feedback. Ensure that your classes are pacey and characterised by efficient use of time.

In teaching 1:1, there may be a danger of 'over-preparation' so keep your eye on the clock and on the student's approach to preparing practice tasks.

With weaker students, or those who are less confident about their language use, you may choose to spend more time on the language in the recorded extracts, using them as models. Some students may benefit from detailed pronunciation work, again using the recordings as models.

Timing: 3 hours

1 Holding the audience's attention

Introduce the discussion through the two opening statements. Elicit students' views on what they mean to them.

Clearly both are concerned with the same thing: the structure of a presentation. Both could equally apply to report-writing and if students have completed Module 2 on telephoning, they may recall seeing the second quotation there. It also applies to correspondence.

1   Have the class discuss the cartoon first. What are the problems here? Clearly the audience, having been bored to their limits, are enjoying a good rest. Ask the students 'Why?' Elicit suggestions such as the talk is far too long, the speaker has not organised the information, her tone is perhaps monotonous, she repeats herself ad nauseam, the content is (perhaps – although we don't know) too technical or too detailed.

2   Move on to the reading text, first discussing the meaning of the title. For your guidance, the title merely suggests that you are not in control of your presentation if the audience are not listening or cannot follow you. The subtitle summarises what is needed.

As with other reading texts, remind students that it is not necessary to read the passage in detail or understand every word.

Ask the students to find six (of the nine) specific recommendations about speaking technique. A highlighter pen is an efficient way to mark the recommendations – or a pencil first and then a highlighter once the correct identification of a point is confirmed.

Key

- Find out about the audience.
- Find out what they need to know.
- Plan what you're going to say.
- Say it clearly and concisely.
- Introduce information using lists.
- Give a link between parts of the presentation.
- Provide a logical sequencing of information.
- Use careful repetition of key information.
- Don't give too much information or too many facts.

Ask students if they have seen – or given – presentations which illustrate the features described here.

Timing: 20 minutes

2 Structure (2) The main body

This section effectively introduces the next three sections.

Introduce the text: it is a statement of key principles in planning and presenting the main body of a presentation.

Use the answers to the questions as a link to other discussion on the text.

Note: There may, of course, be some situations where some of the recommendations do not apply.

Key

a) The main body of the presentation contains the details of what was introduced in the introduction.

b) See figure included in the text.

Timing: 10 minutes

3 Listing information

◻◉ **1** Repeat the point that in both the introduction and the main body of a presentation it is useful to give lists which

signal what you are going to talk about: this guides the audience.

Then introduce the presentations about climatic change. Explain that students will hear *two* versions of the same presentation. They have to say which is the easiest to follow.

Ask for comments on why the **second** version is easier to follow.

- The speaker uses lists to signal what she is going to say.

2 Ask students to look at the tapescript for a couple of minutes and to highlight or underline the key signalling / listing words. See *Tapescript Example 2* for key.

Tapescript

Example 1

… and so climatic changes in the Northern hemisphere may have been the result of volcanic activity. The 1991 eruption may have contributed to ozone damage causing the unusually high world temperatures in 1992.

Also, industrial contamination puts important quantities of noxious gases like CO_2, SO_2, CO and NO_2 into the atmosphere through burning fossil fuels. These gases contribute to the so-called 'greenhouse' effect and global warming. Another main area of industrial pollution of the atmosphere is the release of ozone-damaging chemicals like chlorofluoro-carbons and polychlorobiphenols. These are used in refrigeration, some manufacturing processes and in fire extinguishers. Another source of damage to the environment is car and plane engines because they release the so-called 'greenhouse' gases such as CO_2.

Example 2

… climatic changes in the Northern hemisphere may have been the result of three types of effect on the environment: first, volcanic activity, second industrial pollution, and thirdly transport. Let's look at these in more detail. First, volcanic eruptions. The 1991 eruption may have contributed to ozone damage causing the unusually high world temperatures in 1992. The second key area is industrial contamination.

Industry puts important quantities of noxious gases and chemicals into the atmosphere. <u>There are four important gases</u> released by burning fossil fuels. <u>These are CO_2, SO_2, CO and NO_2.</u> They contribute to the so-called 'greenhouse' effect and global warming. <u>The second main area</u> of industrial pollution of the atmosphere is the release of ozone-damaging chemicals like chlorofluoro-carbons and polychlorobiphenols. These are used in <u>refrigeration, some manufacturing processes and in fire extinguishers. Finally, the third source</u> of damage to the environment is transport. Car and plane engines are a problem because they release the so-called 'greenhouse' gases such as CO_2.

Timing: 15 minutes

Practice 1

The material provided for this exercise – and other practice items in the unit – is optional. Students may prefer to use their own ideas. If you use this situation, first check the vocabulary. Explain the task, point out that the opening words are given and remind students to use listing phrases.

- *Either* allow practice in pairs, then ask individuals to volunteer their efforts *or* have students work individually before presenting to each other in pairs.
- As students practise, provide help and support where necessary.
- Then ask if there were any problems.
- Finally get some individuals to stand up and present their efforts to the class.
- Elicit comment, or give feedback.

When you have heard several students, play the model answer. This may be more complete than the students' versions, but not necessarily better in terms of illustrating the listing technique.

Note: The tapescript is almost entirely composed of phrases introducing lists and the lists themselves. Play the recording again if necessary to get students to focus on the target language. Refer to the Language Checklist.

Timing: 20 minutes

Tapescript

SPEAKER: Good morning, everyone. I'm going to give a brief summary of the transition from export marketing to global marketing. Basically, there are three phases in this transition. These are first export marketing, secondly international marketing and third, global marketing. Let's describe the first phase, which is export marketing.

Export marketing has four main characteristics. First, with export marketing there is home-based production and home-based management. Secondly, there is direct selling to the export markets. Next, it's common to use agents and distributors. Finally, it's possible that there are sales centres in overseas markets. Overall, the investment costs are low with export marketing because almost everything, especially production and management, is still centred on the home base.

Now let's look at the second phase, international marketing. Here I also identify four main characteristics. The first is that production has expanded to overseas markets. This is very important. Next, there is local management. This means you have local cost centres – individually responsible for making a profit. Finally, there is much more local employment of staff, and management. Altogether, this means there is more investment, so investment with international marketing is high.

Now we come to the third phase, which is global marketing. So, global marketing ...Well, at least five main characteristics of the global marketing company. Most important is that the brand name – or brand names – are international, like Kodak or Coca-Cola. Secondly, the brand names

– and the business – is established in all major world markets. This means – and this is the third point – that the business has a 'global identity'. Next, the business has cost centres in all major markets. The fifth and final point, I think, is that the production is often complex, with parts made and transported all over the world between various centres. An example here is a laptop, where perhaps the chips, the circuit board, the case, the screen, the packaging, the documentation, are all made in different locations around the world. Maybe Taiwan, Hong Kong, Singapore, Japan, Brazil and Italy. The result is that the global marketing phase involves very high levels of investment.

That I think – I hope – is a good summary of the stages between export marketing and global marketing. Does anyone have any questions or need clarification on any point?

PHOTOCOPIABLE © Cambridge University Press 2003

4 Linking ideas

1 Introduce the recording as part of the main body of a presentation on energy resources in Latin America, especially Venezuela, Argentina and Peru. For the first playing ask students to identify the main points the speaker makes.

Key

- Venezuela has **oil**.
- Argentina uses **hydro-electric** power and **fossil fuels**.
- Peru has **many resources** but they are **underdeveloped**. Why? **Political** and **economic** factors and Amazon basin is **environmentally sensitive**.

Check that these main points are understood.

2 Play the recording again. Ask students to note the phrases used to link different parts of the presentation, marking the relationship between the 'old' topic and the 'new' one.

Key

a) Let's **look now** at Argentina, which is **quite different from** Venezuela in that it hasn't enjoyed such …
b) That's **all I want to say about** Argentina. Now **let's talk about** Peru.
c) Now, **so much for** Peru. I now want **to say something about** other opportunities in Latin America (*fade*).

3 Elicit alternatives which could be used – see the Language Checklist.

Discuss the benefits of this type of linking:

- it signals to the audience the direction of the content
- it also helps the speaker to keep to the planned structure of the talk

Here is the tapescript with the linking phrases underlined.

Tapescript

SPEAKER: Different countries' energy production is primarily based on their natural resources and their progress in exploiting them.

Now I'd like to talk briefly about Latin America, and three countries in particular, beginning with Venezuela, which for many years has had a strong oil industry. For years the economy has been dependent on oil, and although there are other significant resources in Venezuela, especially water, the emphasis has always been on fossil fuels.

Let's look now at Argentina, which is quite a lot different to Venezuela in that it hasn't enjoyed such a long history of success with oil for the simple reason that they have a great deal less of it. On the other hand, they have developed better use of hydro-electric power, so the use of energy in Argentina has been spread around among many sources – but fossil fuels are once again the most important.

That's all I want to say about Argentina. Now let's talk about Peru.

For many reasons, principally economic, Peru is typical of the Andean countries in that there is far less development of actual resources than such a rich geographical land mass – and a long coast – might lead us to suppose. The Amazon basin is a rich source of very many types of possible energy source. The most important one here is oil, but the problem is, that exploitation of the oil resources conflicts with conservation and ecological responsibilities. And this is a political and economic problem. <u>Now, so much for Peru. I now want to say something about</u> the other opportunities in Latin America …

PHOTOCOPIABLE   © Cambridge University Press 2003

Timing: 15 minutes

Practice 2

Explain that the idea is to present part of a very brief presentation. If students are especially unsure how to use the notes, offer a spontaneous model yourself.

- Remind students to use linking expressions to connect the parts of the talk.
- Stress that what they actually say in terms of content is **not** important: what matters is good use of linking language.
- Topics suggested are optional: learners may choose their own topics.

Stages

- Students choose topics and then work in small groups, where group members have chosen different topics, i.e. they can present to each other in mini-groups.
- They should prepare individually for three to four minutes, then present to each other.

The teacher should:

- provide clarification and assistance as necessary
- monitor the language and offer support.

Follow-up / Feedback:

- one or two volunteers may perform for the class

- give both favourable and critical feedback, taking care to praise good language and good technique.

Timing: 20 minutes

5 Sequencing

Explain that any presentation which describes a process, a schedule or a timetable of events should include examples of sequencing language.
Vocabulary note: A *process* describes how things happen, e.g. how nuclear energy is produced in a pressurised water reactor.
A *schedule* shows when stages happen, e.g. a plan for privatising a state industry.
A *timetable* shows the exact time for a series of events over a short period, e.g. a seminar programme.

1 Introduce the recording as part of a presentation about a construction project in Seoul, South Korea. Play the recording once. Ask students to order the stages of the project.

Key

Put out tenders for construction.	7
Technical consultation to determine design needs.	3
Purchasing procedure.	2
Building.	8
Put out a call for tenders to architects.	4
Select the best proposal.	5
Commission research to find best location for plant.	1
Period of consultation with architects over details.	6

2
Key

- a) First of all
- b) Next
- c) When that's completed
- d) The next step will be
- e) Then
- f) Having chosen
- g) The next stage is

3 Ask students to suggest other examples of similar words and phrases which can be used to explain sequences of events.

Examples are adverbials like *after that, later, finally, the last step is*, as well as ordinal numbers *first, second*, etc. Included above are gerundive expressions with non-finite verbs like *having done that, having completed the tests*, etc. There are also expressions with finite verbs like *once that's done, when we've done that*, etc.

Further practice of sequencing language can be found in the Language Checklist on page 84.

Timing: 15 minutes

Tapescript

SPEAKER: Well, now I'd like to outline the main stages in the project. *First of all* we'll commission research to find out the best location for the plant. *Next* we'll go through the necessary purchasing procedure. *When that's completed* we'll begin technical consultation within the company to determine the exact requirements in the design. *The next step will be* to put out a call for tenders to firms of architects. *Then* we'll select the appropriate proposal. *Having chosen* a design, there'll be a period of intense consultation with the architects over the details. *The next stage is* to put out tenders for the construction of the plant. My guess is that it will take between twelve and eighteen months to reach that point and building won't commence for a further year after that.

Practice 3

Students choose either the given topic or one of their own choice. Give help with vocabulary during preparation. The emphasis should be on sequencing, so remind students to refer to the Language Checklist.

These practice tasks may be individual or group efforts; if time permits, encourage

individuals to present the entire piece alone, even if preparation was a group effort.

A model answer is given on the cassette.

Timing: 20 minutes

Tapescript

SPEAKER: There are six stages in the classical life of a product. These may be extended over any time-scale, maybe a few months for a fashion item or several years for a car or some other consumer durable. First, you have the *development* of the product, then following the development, there is the launch, it is launched in the *introduction* stage and then, the next step is the product gains acceptance and sells, this is the *growth* stage. And then the fourth stage of *maturity* comes next. During this stage, sales peak, reaching the *saturation* point. Having reached a peak, then *decline* sets in. Eventually the product is replaced.

Practice 4

This offers the chance to practise all the language covered by the unit.

- Ask the class to work in pairs to prepare a talk based on the information given.
- Give help where needed, especially to understand the information.
- Remind them to use listing, linking and sequencing where necessary.
- Presentations should be *no longer* than seven minutes.
- Individuals perform for the class.

With a large group, or if you want to allow extra time for an additional run through, allow five minutes' preparation in pairs or groups of three before individuals present to each other and give each other feedback. Then you select some individuals to present a second time to the whole group.

Option: Reproduce the visuals and include them in the presentation.

Timing: 20 minutes

Transfer

This is an opportunity for an informal talk on a topic of each student's choice. Remind them to include a clear introduction and a clear structure. They may also include visual aids.

- Limit preparation (unless set as homework) to ten minutes.
- Limit the presentation itself to seven minutes.
- The presentation should be performed for you and the rest of the group.

Optional Transfer activity

As homework students should prepare the main body of the presentation begun at the end of Unit 6. Suggest looking again at the Checklists in Units 6, 7 and in this unit. For homework, suggest practising the main body, recorded if possible.

When they give the presentation in class, video record each one. With a large class review just a part of each one. Students may view their entire recordings outside class time to see what was good and what should be improved.

Before reviewing, ask for students' reactions to what they have done. (With 1:1 classes, spend more time reviewing the recording.) Play a part of the video with the sound off to check appearance, body language, gesture, eye contact, etc. Then with the sound on, elicit comments and give feedback on:

- clarity and logic of structure, *and then on*
- accuracy of target language (signalling – listing, linking and sequencing).

A note on reviewing audio-recorded presentations
Without the benefit of seeing the presentation, listening to it can make it sound a lot less interesting and often a lot slower than it was in reality. Clearly the disembodied voice of an audio recording is a major distortion of the actual performance. Students may be disturbed by their apparent lack of fluency – with long pauses on the cassette. Often these pauses seem much longer than they appeared to be in reality. It is important to point out this weakness in audio recordings to avoid discouraging the students.

Option

If time permits and you think further practice would be useful, ask students to repeat their presentations to gain improvements as a result of feedback.

- Allow preparation time, then repeat the presentations, recording them again.
- Review the recordings and see if there has been further improvement.

If practical, students might like to have individual videos containing consecutive recordings of their various efforts. This could be useful in terms of demonstrating progress, culminating in a competent and complete presentation.

Skills Checklist

Note: The example breakdown for the main body of a complex presentation could also reflect the structure of a written report. Point this out. Contrast this with a simple three-part main body, with, for example, three key points or a simple chronological structure.

Timing: 10 minutes

9 The end is near ... this is the end

Briefing

This unit completes the examination of the three-part structure of typical presentations. Remember that where speakers of English as a foreign language are concerned, to some extent weakness in language skills can be compensated for by clear structure and good preparation. Conversely, weaknesses in this latter respect will exacerbate communication difficulties which are the result of a less-than-perfect knowledge of English.

Remind students of the need for good planning and sound structure in their presentations. Now is a good time to repeat this point, as students may choose to begin work on a whole new presentation at the end of the module.

A text dealing with questions and discussion offers advice on how to survive what for many speakers can be more difficult than a prepared talk. The unit ends with a light-hearted questionnaire reviewing several aspects of the whole Presentations module. This is on page 73 of the Teacher's Book.

Language focus

The language involved in a discussion following a presentation is in some ways similar to the language of meetings (see Module 4) but there are critical differences. The speaker leading the discussion after a talk is still the focus of attention and is required to respond to comments about the talk itself. The speaker needs to keep control, and can influence the direction of the discussion. However, compared with the presentation itself, the discussion is unstructured. Use the recorded extracts to focus on key phrases and draw attention to the Language Checklist.

1:1 situation

As usual, you may need to prompt discussion and interpretation a little more than with a group class. Take care not to labour the recorded extracts: it is usually a good idea to ask the students if they want to hear extracts one more time. Individuals may welcome the opportunity to use the cassette in self-study for further listening, but warn students not to play extracts not yet used in class.

Timing: 3 hours

1 Structure (3) The end

This is a short section to set the context for the unit. The four questions in this section are designed to stimulate an exchange of suggestions and ideas among the students, getting them to think about this part of a presentation. Elicit ideas, building up discussion. Keep to the point and keep the section brief – 20 minutes maximum.

1 Ask students to brainstorm on what the end of a presentation contains. Elicit any of these:

Key
- recommendations
- summary
- conclusion
- questions
- discussion
- thanks.

Ask whether presentations always end with these items. They almost certainly do not – but in what circumstances and how are the choices made? In business, thanks are fairly standard at the end of a presentation, as are questions.

2 On differences between conclusions and summaries, elicit comments such as:

Key

- *Summaries* restate what has already been said. Remember the maxim: 'In a presentation, say what you are going to say, say it, then tell them you've said it.' Some are like this, but not all.
- A *conclusion* is different: it often contains a message which *grows out* of the information described in the main body of the talk. It may contain lessons learnt, recommendations, next steps.

3 Elicit ideas along these lines:

Key

- The two speakers appear to have a different relationship with the audience. The point is that *inviting questions* assumes that the speaker has specialist knowledge and the audience have come only to listen. Presenters who are experts are very likely to get questions from an audience seeking more information or clarification.
- *Discussion* suggests that the audience / presenter relationship is more equal, *even if it is not*. An audience who have something to add will welcome discussion (as well as the opportunity to ask questions). A discussion is clearly most relevant where theoretical ideas are involved, or where a decision has yet to be made, or plans have to be developed.

4 Elicit suggestions such as:

Key

- Sales rep – questions in most cases (the customer is relatively inexpert).
- Chief executive – questions, depending on who he / she is talking to. It might be a discussion if in a Board meeting.
- Politician's policy speech – typically followed by questions to probe the policy more deeply.
- Team leader's talk – could be either. If it is a

very democratic team, a discussion could be more likely.
- Manager's proposal on improving productivity – probably questions to probe the proposal, discussion to implement or build on it.

A final point could be to elicit views on thanking the audience. Some learners may not be sure how to do this. Elicit / Suggest ways of doing so. Others may feel that it is not necessary in some situations.

Timing: 20 minutes

2 Summarising and concluding

1 Begin by checking understanding of the following key words. Have students look them up in a good business English dictionary, or explain them yourself.

brand name (elicit examples: Coca Cola, Kit Kat, American Express, Pampers)

company valuation – putting a figure on the total assets of a company

assets – something of value

tangible assets – something that can be touched, property, land, stock, finished goods

acquisition – purchase of one company by another (*take over* (v), *takeover* (n))

▭◉ Introduce the recording. Play it once.

Key

Brand names are the key consideration in valuing a company's assets / Brand names are what are important.

▭◉ **2** Play the extract again before checking the answer to the next question.

Key

Both: the first part is a **summary**, the speaker restates the main point, then comes the **conclusion**, containing the speaker's recommendation.

▭◉ **3** Play the recording again if necessary.

Key

'I'd like to **end** with a short **restatement** of the **main point**.'

'So, what are **the lessons** that **we** can **learn** from this? I think most importantly, we **have to** build up … '

Elicit alternative words and phrases that the speaker could have used here.

Language focus option

Comment on the use of rhetorical questions to introduce a conclusion. The example above is a good illustration of this technique, where the speaker asks a question then answers it straightaway. Ask why the rhetorical question is used.

Key

- It appears to involve the audience.
- It highlights the answer – signalling a key point.
- It makes the audience listen.
- It offers variety.

Warning: if overused, it sounds unnatural and irritating.

Elicit / Suggest other ways that speakers can use rhetorical questions in presentations.

Key

- at the beginning
- before key points
- in headings

Tapescript

SPEAKER: So, that brings me to almost the end of my talk. I'd like to end with a short restatement of the main point. The key issue, the key understanding is that it is … in valuing a company's assets, perhaps the key thing these days is the value of brand names. Most acquisitions are in effect attempts to take over brand names. Traditional valuation, based on tangible assets, is no longer sufficient.

So, what are the lessons that we can learn from this? I think most importantly, we have to build up the power of our brand names. We have to establish greater brand identity. This requires a radical approach to marketing, making our brand name the focus of all our efforts. This policy will best boost the company's assets.

Thank you everyone for listening.

Timing: 15 minutes

Practice 1

Set up the context and go through the vocabulary involved. All students should practise once in pairs using the notes for guidance, then volunteers or targeted individuals should stand up to give their version of the summary for the whole class. The summary should last little more than a minute.

Finally, give feedback before playing the model version and eliciting comments or questions.

Timing: 15 minutes

Tapescript

SPEAKER: That concludes the main part of my talk. Now I'd like to summarise the main points. In the past year, three incidents have shown communication problems. In the past five years, 35% of all incidents contained some degree of communication problem.

And finally, we have seen that existing communication procedures are **not** considered satisfactory.

Now, turning to my conclusion, I want to make two key recommendations. Number one, training must place more emphasis on communication procedures. Number two, there should be a programme of regular revision of these communication procedures. And that, ladies and gentlemen, completes my talk.

3 Questions and discussion

📼 ◉ **1** Introduce the recording, the end of a sales presentation by Marisa Repp. She is talking about the Storo, a warehousing system, or a method of storage and retrieval for goods. Explain that students will hear two alternative endings. Play both extracts one after the other.

Key

The first example invites questions; the second invites questions and suggests a discussion.

Tapescript

Example 1

So, I've described how the system works. Now, any questions?

Example 2

I think that covers the main points I wanted to tell you about ... thank you for letting me talk about the Storo System. So ... now ... I'd like to invite you to tell me about the needs that you have ... to suggest any specific qualities you need in a warehousing system ... and at the same time, if there is anything you are not clear about, please ask ... if anything needs clarification.

PHOTOCOPIABLE   © Cambridge University Press 2003

2 Ask for students' suggestions. Any appropriate variations on those given, or those the students are about to hear would be acceptable. You could write students' suggestions on the board, checking accuracy. Note, though, that there is very little wrong with the second example on the recording. It is customer focused. This point is developed in Exercise 3.

📼 ◉ **3** Play the next three extracts.

Key

   a) hard – Example 2
   b) weak – Example 1
   c) soft-sell / customer friendly – Example 3

Tapescript

Example 1

A: So, you can see this is just the kind of insurance you need. Anything you need, we think this policy can do it. Any questions? ... So, no questions? Right, thanks for listening.

Example 2

B: That's it then. A totally integrated networked system ... the best. Now if you've any questions ... I'll be pleased to try to answer them.

C: Yes, I'd like to know ... Is the programming of the computer especially complicated? Can the user make changes easily?

Example 3

D: Now, having told you about the qualities of the machine, I'd like to hear more about how you think a packaging system needs to work to meet your specific situation. Perhaps you could comment on special needs you will have, specially important requirements for effective packing, labelling, special needs ... that sort of thing ...

E: Well, I think the sort of thing we need most ... our most important thing here is flexibility. Our packaging changes a lot ...

PHOTOCOPIABLE   © Cambridge University Press 2003

Timing: 15 minutes

Language focus option

Point out the very direct language used in the hard-sell approach and the economy of 'Any questions?' However, such an approach does not treat the audience as equals.

Contrast this with the weak invitation to questions, which is often inappropriate. It sounds apologetic, almost 'I'm not the right person to talk about this, but ... '. Why does he say he will try to answer the questions? He should say 'Now I'll answer any questions you may have.'

The third example is more cooperative, a more neutral approach, more a soft-sell where he wants to meet the customers' needs.

4 Introduce the text in the usual way, saying total comprehension is not necessary – it is enough to find the problem and three possible solutions.

Key

a) No response from the audience.

b)
- A truly successful and interesting talk will avoid the problem.
- The speaker can give an instruction to the audience – especially in sales presentations.
- To have a question prepared to ask the audience, or identify someone whom you know will have something to say.

Timing: 10 minutes

Discussion option

Spend five minutes eliciting students' views and preferences on these three options. Preferences will probably be different, depending on the type of presentation, the topic, the audience or the situation.

5 Ask students why handling questions and discussion is thought by many speakers to be the most difficult part of a presentation. Difficulties may arise because:

Key
- questions / discussion is relatively unstructured
- the speaker has less control
- speaker has to switch into listen and answer mode
- it may be difficult to hear, to understand, to answer or to distinguish between an opinion and a question.

Then play the recording, introducing it as an experienced speaker talking about handling questions and discussion at the end of a presentation. Ask students to tick the points she mentions.
Discuss these, the other ideas in the book and elicit other ideas from the students.

Key

Be polite.	☐
Listen very carefully.	✓
Ask for repetition or clarification.	✓
Keep calm.	☐
Tell the truth (most of the time!).	✓
Don't say anything you'll regret later.	☐
Check understanding if necessary by paraphrasing.	✓
Agree partially before giving own opinion: 'Yes, but …'	☐

Timing: 15 minutes

Tapescript

INTERVIEWER: So, tell me what you think is the best way to handle questions after a presentation.

PENNY: It's very important to listen very carefully. That's the first thing. Listen. It can be useful to repeat or paraphrase the question, you can check it that way, so you repeat the point the questioner makes. That can help you, it gives you time to think. You must always give yourself time. Also, always ask for clarification if necessary.

INTERVIEWER: What about the answer you give?

PENNY: Well, tell the truth – most of the time!

PHOTOCOPIABLE © Cambridge University Press 2003

6 Introduce the context and play the four extracts one after the other. Play them twice before checking answers:

Key

	Technique	Why?
1	✗	Aggressive, rude, defensive, paranoid
2	✓	Polite, confident and appropriate
3	✗	Badly prepared or not interested
4	✓	Checks, shows partial agreement, makes a related point

Timing: 10 minutes

Language focus option

Play the extracts again to make the above points absolutely clear, focusing on key language, especially in the last example. In all cases, elicit suggestions for what else the speakers could have said.

Tapescript

Extract 1

I didn't get that – or if I did – I can't agree. You're not serious are you? Look, I've been studying this problem for years and I know what I'm talking about.

Extract 2

… And that I think is the real reason for the success of this type of development. Now, if anyone would like to ask a question, I'll be pleased to answer … yes … the gentleman here.

Extract 3

Yes … right, I got your question, but I can't answer it. I've no idea. You'd better ask someone else.

Extract 4

Yes, I think I follow you. Are you saying that there used to be more government support, but now this is more difficult? Yes … that's true, but there's something else to say about government grants … these are often not widely publicised, not everyone knows what is available … there may be tax advantages …

PHOTOCOPIABLE © Cambridge University Press 2003

Practice 2

This exercise can be done in pairs, individually, in class or as homework or a self-study option. Check students' suggestions. Model answers are given here. Read these, or suggest others.

1 So, that concludes what I want to say, so now I'd like to ask you for your comments, opening up discussion, or perhaps you have a question or two?

2 Er, in fact what I said was this process has been going on for a very long time. I'm sorry if I was not clear on this point.

3 I wonder if anyone can suggest why this has happened or if anyone has any comments on it?

4 Yes, you're right, but can I suggest one or two other factors? One is the increasing number of takeovers of smaller companies …

5 So are you saying that in the USA or Europe that could not happen?

6 Yes, I agree, but the situation *is* changing.

7 Sorry, I don't quite follow you. Can you say that again … put it another way … ?

Timing: 15 minutes

Practice 3

This exercise involves presenters and an audience. Make sure that the purpose of the exercise is clear. It is to give practice, mainly to the presenter, but also to the audience, in dealing with the questions and discussion after a presentation.

- Students should work in groups, ideally of four, but three or five will work.
- First, all group members need to prepare their presentations.
- Encourage them to choose topics they know well and can talk about fairly easily, even if it is not work or business-oriented.
- Once everyone is ready, a volunteer should take 'the hot seat' (and stand up!) to deliver their short extract.
- At the end, the speaker moves to discussion / invites questions, etc. and the other group members have to respond accordingly.
- Remind the audiences to listen carefully: the exercise will not work without audience participation. However, if the audience is not forthcoming, the speaker will have to cajole them into asking questions or ask questions, so stimulating audience / speaker interaction.

Note: Record this if you and the group want to. Once the activity starts, you should be alert to see if it is struggling or flagging. You may be able to interject with questions yourself, especially ones that put the speaker on the spot: ask a totally incomprehensible question, or say something quite the opposite to what the speaker actually said.

With a 1:1 class, you should play an entire audience.

Timing: 30 minutes

Transfer

Get students to prepare this for homework. Actually presenting their efforts in class should not take much more than a minute or two per student, but make sure that each contribution is given some useful feedback, either praise or constructive criticism.

Note: As a general rule, where criticism is involved, first elicit the student's comments on what he / she thought and how it could be better. Then add your own comments and suggestions.

Optional Transfer activity

Give students time (preferably as homework or self-study) to prepare the final part of the presentation they have been working on in Units 6, 7 and 8. Remind them to pay special attention to a summary or a conclusion or both. Encourage separate practice of the final part of the presentation.

- They should also prepare for questions.
- Ask them to try to anticipate likely questions from their audience.
- They should also think of one or two questions to ask them.

Once they have prepared the end they are almost in a position to give their complete presentations. Suggest they look again at the Checklists in this module.

Finally students give their presentations. Record them on audio or video cassette if possible. Questions and/or discussion should follow.

Limit each presentation to 10–15 minutes.

Before playing the recording, ask students how they think it went. Ask:

- what were the positive things
- what could be improved.

If you have video-recorded the presentation, play **part** of it without the sound. Ask students to consider the appearance. Is the presenter relaxed and confident? Does he/she keep eye contact and look friendly and interested?

Play the recording with the sound. Elicit students' assessments and give feedback in terms of the points referred to in the Student's Book.

Skills Checklist

Use the Checklist to reaffirm some of the principles discussed in this unit. Give the students time to ask any questions or raise any points they want to discuss.

Some implications of the points included here require further discussion. Look in particular at the *Handling questions* section. Discuss any recommendations or suggestions which have not featured until now in class discussions. Where appropriate, ask students what they would say to overcome a particular difficulty (e.g. being asked an irrelevant question, or not knowing how to answer).

Remind them that the Checklist is a resource for them to refer to later during preparation of presentations.

Timing: 10 minutes

Presentation technique: a self-check

This is a light-hearted look at various visual aspects of presentations and can be photocopied (see Teacher's Book page 73) and used as an additional resource at the end of the Presentations module. Check answers in class with the key.

Presentation technique: checking the answers

Students can do this alone or in pairs. Check answers or opinions, hearing from various learners. Aim to reach a consensus on each point. Add comments from below:

a) 1. But there could be occasions when a speaker would prefer to sit down – at least for part of the presentation, e.g. a presentation to a very small audience, or in some meetings or negotiations.

b) 2. Usually a podium restricts movement, but one might decide not to use it.

c) 4. Movement is often very useful and desirable.

d) 2. Depends on culture and individual style, but in most professional situations it would be normal to wear a tie.

e) 5. You should always look at the audience and at different people.

f) 5. Certainly not! In most cases, personal anecdotes about family and friends are not relevant to a formal or semi-formal presentation.

g) 1. Yes, but you should probably also check it yourself!

h) 2. Yes, probably – using a pointer. However in many cases a small pointer directly on the OHP (and so visible as a shadow on the screen) is very effective. It's best to test the room and the equipment and see which is most suitable. If the screen is a few metres behind the speaker, which it may be in a conference hall, pointing at the screen is impossible anyway.

i) 3. Depends on nature of picture. Many speakers don't like this technique. Audiences may be distracted, thinking 'I wonder what I can't see?'

j) 5. No – unfortunately it is almost always a weakness. However, some speakers (e.g. politicians) are good at concealing that they are reading, but it takes a lot of practice. Good presenters often use cue cards or nothing.

k) 1. Yes, but make sure there's enough eye contact. Occasionally pausing to refer to notes is often useful, helping the speaker *and* giving the audience time to assimilate information.

l) 4. Depends on the audience, the subject, the situation, etc. Cultural differences and the problem that jokes don't translate make joke-telling risky. The following story is apocryphal: A British salesman went to Japan to present his product. He spoke no Japanese and the audience spoke no English so he hired an interpreter. In the middle of the presentation he told a joke. The audience laughed appreciatively. After the presentation the British guy felt very pleased and said to the interpreter: 'They liked my joke. How exactly did you translate it?' The interpreter replied 'I thought there's no way a Japanese audience will understand that kind of humour so I said to them "The Englishman has just told a joke. It would be polite if you all laughed"'. Humour at the start of a presentation may be appropriate. Here is a nice example: 'Hello. You are going to listen to me. I'm going to talk to you for about 20 minutes. If you finish before I do, please let me know.'

m) 1. Yes, it can!

n) 2. Possibly, some of the time. If you're a woman wearing a dress with no pockets, you can't anyway!

o) 1. Almost certainly true.

p) 4. There is an element of performance – but no, it's not acting.

q) 4. More speed = worse control, less audience comprehension. Select the most important of your remaining points and say that. Also, plan better next time!

r) 5. PowerPoint is a brilliant tool for presentations, but it needs careful preparation, thought and practice. Always check the equipment first.

Presentation technique: a self-check

Mark the following statements on a scale of 1 to 5:

1 = 'I agree entirely'   2 = 'I usually agree'   3 = 'I have no opinion / I'm not sure'

4 = 'I usually disagree'   5 = 'I disagree entirely'

a)	Speakers giving a presentation should always stand up.	1 2 3 4 5
b)	Speakers should not move around if there is a podium.	1 2 3 4 5
c)	Speakers should not move around at all.	1 2 3 4 5
d)	Men giving formal presentations should always wear a tie.	1 2 3 4 5
e)	You should never look at the audience – it frightens them.	1 2 3 4 5
f)	Tell personal anecdotes about your family and friends to get the audience's attention.	1 2 3 4 5
g)	You should always check with the organisers that all the equipment works.	1 2 3 4 5
h)	When showing overhead transparencies you should always point at the screen, not at the transparency.	1 2 3 4 5
i)	When using transparencies, use cards to cover up any parts that you do not want the audience to see.	1 2 3 4 5
j)	Reading from a script is okay.	1 2 3 4 5
k)	Using notes is fine.	1 2 3 4 5
l)	You can tell jokes to relax your audience.	1 2 3 4 5
m)	Seeing yourself on video can reveal irritating habits like shaking money in your pocket.	1 2 3 4 5
n)	Putting both hands in your pockets is wrong but one hand is okay.	1 2 3 4 5
o)	Speakers often feel more nervous than they look.	1 2 3 4 5
p)	A good presentation is a performance – you need to be an actor.	1 2 3 4 5
q)	If you are running out of time, speak more quickly.	1 2 3 4 5
r)	You don't need to think about technique if you use PowerPoint.	1 2 3 4 5

Discuss the implications of the questions and your answers with colleagues.

10 Making meetings effective

AIMS
- What makes a good meeting?
- Chairing a meeting
- Establishing the purpose of a meeting

Briefing

This unit begins with a look at the characteristics of effective meetings and emphasises good preparation. Remind students that if a planned meeting will be in English, then preparation should also be in English.

A principle underlying the unit is that good leadership is essential to the success of most meetings.

Throughout the unit, encourage students to give their opinions, reminding them – if necessary – that everyone has experience of meetings of one sort or another.

There is opportunity for leading discussion and practising the functions involved in chairing. Some students may feel they will never chair meetings or lead discussions, but most professionals will probably lead discussions at some time. In fact, students' reluctance may have more to do with their feeling insufficiently competent to lead a discussion in English. The unit aims to develop exactly this competence. Later units in the module give more attention to language functions employed in meetings. Here, the role play should be a fluency exercise without detailed study of the language functions which feature more prominently in Unit 11.

Language work

You may use the Practice exercise and the Role play to include more language content. If you record these tasks then feedback can be more detailed, but taking a few notes and making comments in feedback may be sufficient. Too much analysis could be demotivating – especially with group classes.

1:1 situation

The unit works effectively in 1:1 teaching. Naturally, there will be a heavier onus on you to prompt suggestions, and to make suggestions yourself. In the role play discussions, you will need to participate fully. However, the earlier parts of the unit focus on preparation and the language of chairing. These sections can be used effectively in 1:1 teaching.

Timing: 3.5 hours

1 What makes a good meeting?

Encourage consideration of the definition quoted from Gower in relation to the illustrations which show a variety of meetings, large, small, formal and informal.

The second quotation, 'The fewer the merrier', needs more explanation. It is a corruption of 'the more the merrier', used about social contexts such as parties. Explain *merrier* as derivative of *merry (happy)*. Ask why Frank says this about meetings. What point is he making? He is concerned about efficiency in decision-making. To save time, only people who are really necessary should be invited. Long meetings are often the least effective.

In terms of preparation, have students think about *the purpose* and *the type* of the meeting, and *who* should be invited.

Discuss types of meeting. Ask the students to suggest what types there are and what kind they have been involved in. Get them to say if they were good or bad meetings and why. Focus the discussion by eliciting or suggesting three types:

- information-giving
- discussion meetings
- decision-making meetings.

1 Have students work in pairs, writing notes for about a minute. Then hear suggestions from various pairs, widening discussion to the group. Possible suggestions are listed here but if these are not forthcoming, suggest a few of them only after the listening task which follows. You do not have to mention them all – some are perhaps obvious.

Key

- good preparation
- good chairing
- not too many people
- all views represented
- polite discussion
- consensus of opinion
- clear objective(s)
- objective(s) reached in the time stipulated
- good planning of resources and equipment
- social element if the meeting is with people from outside the company
- refreshments as appropriate.

🔲 ◎ 2 Introduce the recording of Allan Case, an engineer, talking about the characteristics of successful business meetings. Play the tape twice. Students should identify which five of the eight points below are made by the speaker and order them, 1–5.

Key

There is a written agenda.	–
Clear objectives – known to everyone.	2
Respect for the time available / time-planning.	5
Good chair – effective control.	3
Emotions are kept under control.	–
Good preparation.	1
Everyone gets to say what they need to say.	–
Reaching objectives.	4

Elicit further comments and any comments on the three points *not* made by Allan Case.

Key

- The point about a written agenda is perhaps valid for pre-arranged formal meetings, but for emergency meetings or for informal situations the agenda may not be written down. It is important though that there are clear and well-understood objectives: these in fact are the agenda.
- That everyone gets to say what they need to say can be subsumed under the phrase 'good chair – effective control'. The word *need* is important.
- *Usually* it is best to keep emotions under control. Speakers make their points best if they use self-control, are objective and avoid personal or subjective argument.

Tapescript

INTERVIEWER: What do you see as the most important characteristics of a successful meeting?

ALLAN CASE: I think it's important that everyone is well prepared. Certainly everyone should prepare for the meeting – which is possible in all cases except emergency meetings where there's no time for much preparation.

A second point is that in every case, people should understand the objectives of the meeting. Also, the role of the chair is important. The chair should do a good job, keep control and keep the meeting focused on the objectives. That means the meeting reaches its aims.

INTERVIEWER: And what about the timing of the meeting?

ALLAN CASE: Yes, I agree, the meeting should keep to the timing – start and finish on time. That's also important.

Timing: 30 minutes

2 Chairing a meeting

As a brief introduction, ask students to brainstorm for two minutes on the functions of the chairperson in a meeting. Write ideas on the board. Leave their suggestions visible until after they have heard the recorded extract which follows.

⊞ ◎ **1** Introduce the recording. It is part of a meeting at a subsidiary of a multinational company. Play the extract once and ask students to identify reasons for the fall in profits.

Key

Prices are too high.	No
The company has wasted money on research and development.	No
Sales are down.	Yes
The sales budget is too low.	Yes
No one likes the Chief Sales Executive.	No
The products are old.	Yes

⊞ ◎ **2** Play the extract again. Ask students to think only about the role of the chair. Ask them to identify which functions of the chair are illustrated in this extract, i.e. Does he do any of the following? Which? They can do this individually, then compare with each other, before listening again to check their answers.

Key

Thanks people for coming.	☐
Prevents interruptions.	☑
Starts the meeting on time.	☑
Makes people stick to the subject.	☐
States the objective.	☑
Gives his own opinion.	☐
Refers to the agenda.	☑
Summarises.	☑
Changes the agenda.	☐
Asks for comments.	☑
Talks about a previous meeting.	☐
Decides when to have a break.	☐
Introduces the first speaker.	☑
Closes the meeting.	☐

Elicit still more functions of the chair, for example, to move the discussion on, focus discussion, thank speakers, fix next meeting, assign roles, etc.

3 Choose whether to do this exercise orally with the whole class, or to have learners work in pairs. The phrases may be written down as a self-study or homework exercise. Possible answers are given here. For items with an asterisk (*), see Language focus option below.

Key

a) Welcome, everybody. Thank you for coming.

b) We are here today to talk about … (and to decide …)*

c) We have an agenda with three points.*

d) I think Mr Kano is ready to tell us something about … *

e) If you don't mind, can we let Mr Kano finish?*

f) Thank you for that …

g) Now, can I ask Ms Perez de Sanchez to tell us her views …

h) Er, can we try to keep to the topic – I think we have gone away from it a little.

i) I'd like to sum up the main points.*

j) Would anyone like to say anything else on this?*

k) I think we ought to move on to the next topic on the agenda.

l) So, before the next meeting, I'll send out a report on this one, Mr Kano will prepare (…) and we will then fix a new date, some time next month.

m) Thank you. That's everything. That's it for today.

Note: Refer students to the Language Checklist. Check understanding of all the phrases given, including those relating to apologies and the minutes of a previous meeting. These have not been dealt with so far.

Language focus option

For the six phrases marked * above, an alternative answer is contained in the tapescript. Photocopy and distribute the tapescript. Have students check if any of their suggestions match what is in the tapescript. Can they identify the six alternatives?

Key
- Well, we're here today to look at …
- You've all seen the agenda. (I'd like to ask if anyone has any comments on it.)
- Can I ask (…) to open with his remarks.
- Sorry, (…), I can't allow us to consider that question just yet …
- So let me summarise that. You say that …
- Does anyone have anything to add to that?

Pronunciation option

Read the model answers above to the class to provide pronunciation models. Have students repeat them, copying your intonation.

Note: h) begins with the hesitation sound, or filler, *Er.* This is common in English before a critical remark. Without it, it could sound aggressive or impatient. There is an example of this on the tapescript as well. If you like, play the recording again to get students to identify it.

Tapescript

BERNARD:	Okay, I think we should start now, it's 10 o'clock.
VOICES:	Right.
BERNARD:	Well, we're here today to look at some of the reasons for the decline in profits which has affected this subsidiary. You've all seen the agenda. I'd like to ask if anyone has any comments on it before we start?
VOICES:	No.
BERNARD:	Right, well, can I ask Sam Canning, Chief Sales Executive, to open up with his remarks.
SAM:	Thank you, Bernard. Well I think we have to face up to several realities and what I have to say is in three parts and will take about 20 minutes.
BERNARD:	Er, Sam … we don't have much time – it's really your *main* points we're most interested in.
JANE:	Yes, can I ask one thing, Mr Chairman? Isn't this a global problem in our market?

BERNARD:	Sorry, Jane, I can't allow us to consider that question just yet. We'll look at the global question later. Sam, sorry, please carry on.
SAM:	Well, the three points I want to make can be made in three sentences. First, sales are down, but only by 5% more than for the group as a whole. Secondly, our budget for sales has been kept static – it hasn't increased – not even with inflation – so we're trying to do better than last year on less money. Thirdly –
JANE:	That's not exactly true …
BERNARD:	Jane, please. Let Sam finish.
SAM:	Thirdly, the products are getting old – we need a new generation.
BERNARD:	So let me summarise that. You say that sales are down but not by so much, that you've had less money to promote sales and that the products are old? Is that right?
SAM:	In a nutshell.
BERNARD:	Does anyone have anything to add to that?
JANE:	Well on the question of funding I have to disagree.

Timing: 35 minutes

Language focus option

Refer to the Language Checklist, go through it with the class, especially to check pronunciation. Remind students that the Language Checklist offers just a few of the phrases that could be used. While students should be familiar with the expressions featured, they should only use ones they feel comfortable with.

Pronunciation option

Intonation

Use the recording as an illustration of how English has falling intonation in affirmative sentences (there are many examples) especially where one is handing over to another speaker.

There are also two good examples of rising intonation in yes / no questions (Is that right? Does anyone have anything to add to that?).

Note that Jane's first interruption, while having the *form* of a question (Can I ask … ?) is not a genuine question, so it does not have rising intonation.

Word stress
Key words are stressed at several points in this extract and a good example is in Sam's contribution.

Right. Thanks. Well, the **three** points I want to make I can make in **three** sentences. First, sales **are** down, but only by 5% **more** than for the group as a **whole**. Secondly, our budget for sales has been kept **static** – it hasn't increased – not even with inflation – so we're trying to do **better** than last year on **less** money …

… Thirdly, the products are getting **old** – we **need** a **new** generation.

In the last sentence he stresses several words for extra emphasis.

You could also point out that he stresses *First*, *Secondly*, and *Thirdly*, to highlight the structure of what he is saying.

You could use the Tapescript to have students practise reading this dialogue aloud, emphasising some of the features described here.

Practice 1

This should be a light-hearted and lively exercise. Impress on students that the *content* of what they say is not important so only very little preparation is required. The eventual practice should last only about ten minutes: the idea is to get the chair to use as much of the language for chairing a meeting as possible, including controlling a meeting, moving the discussion along, changing speaker, dealing with interruptions, etc.
Procedure
First choose either Situation 1 or 2. If there is time later, do them both.

Then decide who will be chairs and call them As. There should be as many As as there can be groups of four in the class, i.e. three in a class of 12.

Nominate all the other learners as Bs, Cs and Ds. Bs should present proposals for item 1 on the agenda, Cs for item 2 and Ds for item 3.

All chairs (As) should prepare together what they will do. All Bs should prepare their ideas together, all Cs and Ds likewise.

After five minutes, they should form groups consisting of one of each A, B, C, and D and the chairs should immediately get the meetings started.

Tell the chairs they must get through the agenda in ten minutes, hearing the proposals from all three contributors.

In Situation 1 tell Bs to argue that item 1 has to be decided before items 2 and 3 otherwise the meeting is a waste of time. Tell Cs and Ds to argue for preferred choices of country and to choose a preferred medium for advertising. This should guarantee a lively meeting and keep the chair busy. Limit the discussion to ten minutes.

Limit the meetings to ten minutes.

Options

One way to extend this and to have more students practise the role of chair is to interrupt after ten minutes – when the chair in each meeting should in any case have got through the three items on the agenda – and suggest a discussion covering all three proposals on the agenda. Appoint a new chair in each group to control the discussion and end the meeting.

An alternative is to repeat the exercise with different groups and with different roles, especially different chairs. Either use the same topic, or the alternative, or another one that you or the students choose.

Timing: 20 minutes or 40 minutes if repeated

3 Establishing the purpose of a meeting

All meetings should have an agenda and the objectives of the meeting should be clear. The word 'agenda' is used here in a broad sense, comprising formal, written agendas as well as informal, understood, shared objectives. An example of the latter could be a meeting called in response to a particular emergency.

1 Play the recording twice, then check the information needed to complete the agenda (underlined in the tapescript).

Key

a) Budget for present projects
b) The future outlook
c) Funding alternatives

Tapescript

VICTOR: Okay, I think we should begin. Thanks for coming – and as you know – this is … we're here for our ERU Quarterly meeting. As you know from the agenda there are three main issues to discuss. The first is to review the <u>budget for present projects</u> – Hydroclear and PCB reduction.

Secondly, we'll look at <u>the future outlook</u> for the Unit. Finally, we'll examine the money question, <u>funding alternatives</u>. So – any comments, any suggestions, or is everyone happy with that agenda? Okay, then let's start with item one on the agenda. I think Professor Camden has prepared a statement on the Hydroclear budget, so I'll hand over to him.

VINCE: Thank you, Mr Chairman. Well, with the Hydroclear project, I would like to summarise the crisis on funding: each year we have higher costs and the money coming in to support the project is less. I have produced a report on the main choices.

PHOTOCOPIABLE © Cambridge University Press 2003

C Inc.

Corolla Inc. 222 Santa Monica Blvd
Pasadena CA 91101 USA
www.corollainc.com

John Senna
Corolla Expo
42–48 Maddison Square
Sacramento CA 85400
USA

August 21, 20—

Dear John

As you know we have recently been examining alternatives to the Hacienda model which is now reaching maturity in its life cycle. We need to plan a successor before the range enters decline.

I am planning a regional meeting to look at alternatives and the most likely date is October 21–22, here in Pasadena. I enclose a provisional agenda. Please let me know if you can attend and if you have any comments on the agenda.

We will send you more details nearer the time and perhaps you could call if you want me to arrange anything to help you in your contributions to the meeting.

Looking forward to seeing you again.

Yours truly,

J.B.Black
Vice-President Marketing

PHOTOCOPIABLE © Cambridge University Press 2003

Practice 2

1 Working in groups of (ideally) four, students have to prioritise the given items and decide on an appropriate agenda for the meeting.
   - Each group should actually write out the agenda.
   - Groups then exchange agendas.
   - Ask them to note any differences: this can lead to discussion, with groups justifying their preferred order on their agenda.
      See model answer below.

2 Once the agenda has been agreed, students should work in pairs to create a satisfactory opening statement by the chair of the meeting.

Note:

- This is principally the chair's opening address, but could include a brief reference to absences and the acceptance of the minutes of the previous meeting. You will need to help students with this.
- Refer again to the Language Checklist.
- The opening address by Victor Allen on the recording can serve as a short illustration of what is needed.
- Some students may be competent and confident enough to build more into the chair's opening address, including some kind of appraisal. This is strictly optional.

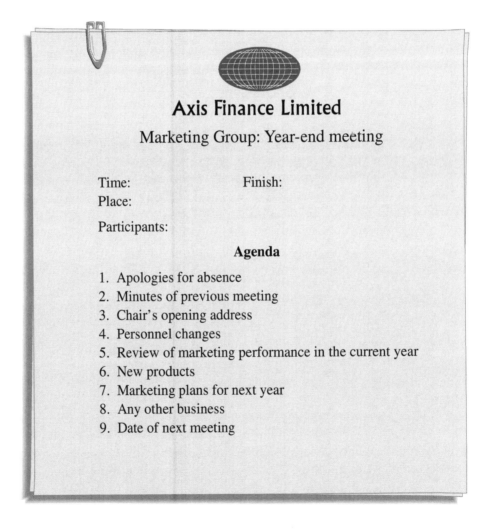

Axis Finance Limited

Marketing Group: Year-end meeting

Time: Finish:
Place:

Participants:

Agenda

1. Apologies for absence
2. Minutes of previous meeting
3. Chair's opening address
4. Personnel changes
5. Review of marketing performance in the current year
6. New products
7. Marketing plans for next year
8. Any other business
9. Date of next meeting

One way to develop this exercise is to have pairs split up and find someone else to work with, just to present their prepared opening statements. They should be able to do this with minimal written support: the agenda, perhaps with minimal notes added, should be sufficient. You listen to some students practising and give them support.

Finally, get one or two volunteers to offer their opening remarks for the whole class to hear. Elicit comment and give general feedback to the group.

Timing: 20 minutes

Writing option

Possible group work (collaborative writing) or individual homework or self-study task. Students may write a letter informing other class members of a forthcoming meeting, inviting them to attend and enclosing a copy of an agenda.

Check students' work, indicating errors and suggesting improvements. Later, also for homework, ensure that they rewrite their letter as a perfect 'model version'.

There is an example of such a letter on page 79.

Role play

Set up the role play by reading through the introductory paragraph. Explain anything which is not clear.

Before they start, it is important that you stress the three teaching / learning objectives:

1 To practise the language of chairing a meeting and leading discussion, including introducing topics, bringing in other speakers, asking for comments, etc., controlling the meeting, summarising, etc.

2 Fluency practice: to speak freely on a range of topics, express opinion, talk in English!

3 The objective in the discussion is to decide on a recommendation to give to the Board.

Ask individuals to look **briefly** at all four File cards 20–23 and to choose **one** on which they want to lead discussion. In five minutes' preparation, they should study their choice and prepare to introduce that item on the agenda by outlining the key facts. They may like to refer to the Language Checklist during preparation.

Obviously this works best with four or five students per group. The fifth can be the overall chair of the discussion. If there are fewer than five and one of the group in particular wishes to practise chairing meetings then he / she can have a dual role as overall chair and leader of the discussion on one of the topics. If there are eight or more students, divide the class into groups or have students work in pairs to co-present and co-lead a topic. Your decisions on this will probably be dictated by space availability.

Students need to fully understand the opening paragraph, the logistics of the task as well as the details of their chosen topic. They may also build on these details, providing additional information.

Recording option

Record the meeting. This will add a degree of extra pressure to the role play, so helping to get students to use the exercise as a serious practice activity. In most cases the content of the discussion will be far removed from students' actual meetings, but the conduct and language of the meeting should mirror professional situations. Provide selected feedback, do not attempt to give detailed feedback on the entire meeting. You should concentrate on the effectiveness with which individuals introduced the topics and led discussion.

1:1 situation

For the role play, if you work in an institution where several 1:1 classes are run simultaneously, there may be an opportunity to bring participants together for this meeting. Individuals can prepare for the meeting and, though some general feedback looking at the general success or otherwise of the discussion would naturally be appropriate, detailed feedback for each individual on his / her contributions can be given in the 1:1 class.

The meeting itself should be restricted to a maximum of 40–45 minutes.

If such a combination is not possible, the role play situations can still form the basis of discussion between you and the student. You should perhaps lead discussion on one topic, thus providing a model of how to approach each issue, before inviting the student's comments and suggestions and together reaching a consensus. Then ask the student to lead discussion on the other topics, summarising the issues involved, then asking for your views, then adding his / her own and drawing a consensus from what is said.

Timing: 1 hour

Writing options

Anyone in the group with a special interest in writing or note-taking may like to practise taking minutes during the meeting. He / She should check notes with the discussion leaders and / or the chair afterwards.

A further option is for one individual to produce a memo recording the recommendations decided upon and give this to all participants. A further option is for each discussion leader to produce a memo recording the result of the discussion on his / her topic and distribute this among other members of the class.

Memos should include the main points from the discussion and the decision on what recommendation should be made to the Board of Ash & Whitebeam.

Transfer 1

The Transfer tasks in this unit can be set as optional homework, or worked on in class individually or in small groups.

The aim is that students evaluate the Ash & Whitebeam meeting in a realistic manner. In doing so, they can assess what they have learned from the unit as a whole and what further improvement is needed. So, treat the Transfer tasks as flexibly as you feel is appropriate. Try to get a broad evaluation of what students have achieved from the unit, if you like going beyond the Ash & Whitebeam meeting to include the other practice tasks as well.

Once students have prepared their responses, you can spend 10–15 minutes discussing their impressions.

Option: For students who are already in work you could instead adapt the Transfer to an evaluation of an actual meeting that they have taken part in.

Transfer 2

This is an optional opportunity to focus again on the role of the chair. As above, individual students can do this as homework and report back in class.

Transfer 3

This Transfer is specifically for students who are planning to take part in an actual meeting. It focuses on preparation for meetings.

11 Sorry to interrupt, but ...

AIMS
- The structure of decision-making
- Interrupting and handling interruptions
- Stating and asking for opinion

Briefing

The unit opens with a reading text on the structure of decision-making. There are two models of meeting structure presented in this unit. One is in the opening reading text on decision-making meetings. The other, the so-called DESC model, is included in the Skills Checklist.

There is plenty of opportunity for discussion, including several topics of general interest, outside the business context of the course.

The functional areas covered are dealt with using three recorded extracts from meetings as well as practice tasks. These prepare the ground for a substantial role play activity which will require some preparation, especially in terms of vocabulary.

Language focus

The target language is widely illustrated in the three recorded extracts and the practice tasks provide opportunity to use this language. Of course, there are many alternative ways that opinions can be expressed and interruptions made. It is important that students are encouraged to experiment outside the language presented here, but they should learn to recognise the language heard in the extracts and included in the Language Checklist. As always, the unit aims to develop confidence in using a range of language suitable for the target areas of the unit.

1:1 situation

As in other units, in the 1:1 situation you need to be ready to participate more directly in discussions.

There are many topics suggested for discussion. You should allow students plenty of choice in selecting topics to discuss. Allow a few moments for students to gather their thoughts and ideas.

Timing: 3.5 hours

1 The structure of decision-making

Ask the class to suggest three different kinds of meeting. Refer to the Skills Checklist in Unit 10 if necessary. Elicit the following:
- information-giving meetings
- discussion meetings
- decision-making meetings.

Ask them which kind is most likely to be the subject of the cartoon which opens the unit (probably a discussion meeting). With the three types of meeting in mind, students should move on to look at the text.

1 **Key**
  a) Decision-making meetings.
  b) The structure of decision-making: see the bulleted points in the second paragraph.
  c) Communication has to be a two-way process to be successful.

2
  a) Students should say that not all meetings are to make a decision – as implied in the first sentence of the text. Decisions may already have been made, so a meeting is called to tell people about the decision (an information-giving meeting).
  b) Perhaps less contentious: check that students understand the steps outlined in the text.

They may have other ideas. In fact, an alternative description of the structure of decision-making is the DESC model, which is included in the Skills Checklist. Refer to that and have students compare the two models.

c) Again, this may be contentious. In many instances of communication, a message is given and it is sufficient that it is comprehended, without even an acknowledgement (a recorded message, for example). However, this may be splitting hairs: the point is that in meetings at least an acknowledgement or agreement is expected. It seems fair to say that in most cases, communication is a two-way process.

d) It is true that often an agreement, or consensus, can be arrived at without a formal vote: it is the leader's responsibility to make clear what the consensus is and ask if everyone accepts it.

Note: Some students may find part of the first paragraph confusing. Ask what *this* refers to in line 3 (→ consensus). Then either elicit or explain the meaning of *the most time- and cost-effective manner.* It is important to recognise that it means *time-effective* and *cost-effective.*

3 Possible self-study or homework task.

Key

    a) consensus
    b) time- and cost-effective manner
    c) goal
    d) set an objective
    e) imperatives
    f) desirables
    g) evaluate alternatives
    h) perception
    i) awareness / empathy
    j) evolve
    k) verbalise

Timing: 20 minutes

2 Stating and asking for opinion

1 Prompt a two-minute brainstorm on ways of stating opinion, writing them on the board. Here are some possible answers:

Key
I think / believe / reckon / feel / guess …
In my experience / view / opinion …
As I see it … / It seems to me … / I'd say …
My view / idea / guess / opinion / belief / thinking is that …

2 Introduce the recording and the picture accompanying it. Have the class look at the three questions, then play the recording once.

Key
    a) They are very similar.
    b) B.
    c) A. Company A has better market prospects.

3 Check the answers to *a* and *b* together by playing the recording through and pausing after each relevant phrase.

Key
    a) Asking for opinion:
      So?
      Any thoughts?
      What do you think about that?
      What about … ?
      Mary?
    b) Stating opinion:
      Yes, but I'm fairly sure …
      I'm sure …
      We're confident that …

Note: These each contain an element of toning down. Point this out. Also, point out that many opinions are expressed in the extract without introductory phrases like 'I think', 'My view is', 'In my opinion.'

Language focus and pronunciation option

Spend a little more time on eliciting phrases for stating opinion. Refer to ways to express opinion more strongly or weakly. This can be illustrated by offering models to show how pronunciation (especially intonation, pausing and stress) can affect the degree of belief a speaker has in what he / she is saying:

'I **think** the price is too high' compared with
'**I** think the price is | **too** high'.
(| = pause)

Timing: 20 minutes

Tapescript

ALEX: Well, first of all, I'll talk about the technical features of the two systems, just in terms of their capabilities …

GEORGE: No details, Alex, please.

ALEX: No, in fact it couldn't be easier … they're practically identical.

GEORGE: So?

ALEX: There's no real difference between them – not in terms of use or performance.

GEORGE: Mary, any thoughts?

MARY: No, I agree, technically they are almost the same.

ALEX: So the next consideration is price. A is certainly more expensive. All A products are quite a lot dearer, we're talking about 10 to 15%.

GEORGE: And what do you think about that?

ALEX: Price isn't everything.

GEORGE: Hmm …

ALEX: A has a technical lead in research and a growing market share.

MARY: But a smaller share right now.

ALEX: Yes, but I'm fairly sure A looks a stronger company in the long term.

GEORGE: So, what about B, then?

MARY: Well, a larger market share, a lot cheaper, we know that, but if our market analysis is right, this will change.

GEORGE: But to summarise, you think that A will do better, er … has more potential to survive future commercial pressures?

ALEX: I'm sure the company has an excellent future, good design, good marketing strategy.

MARY: Yes, absolutely. Everything we found out leads us to the same conclusion, even though the price is higher, the name less well known, we're confident that A is a better solution.

GEORGE: Alex?

ALEX: That's right, we have to look ahead …

PHOTOCOPIABLE © Cambridge University Press 2003

Practice 1

Explain that this involves asking for opinion on a range of topics and giving your own opinion, in various ways, depending on your feelings. Explain that students should stand and walk around asking various colleagues about *any* one of the topics. Then they should go on to ask *someone else* about *another* of the topics. In this way, the exercise is kept active, with plenty of movement and short exchanges. Naturally, students can come back to ask the same person again about another topic, but preferably only after talking to someone else, including you, the teacher. Students should briefly note the answers they get.

Once everyone has conducted around 12–15 mini-interviews, get the students to return to their seats. Go through the topics eliciting individuals' estimates of the views of the group. Ask others to comment, affirming or modifying it according to their findings. In this way the class should be able to build up a picture of the balance of opinion on each topic and the strength of conviction.

1:1 situation

The exercise can be done with a 1:1 class where you and the student exchange opinions. It may be possible to add to this by talking to other English speakers outside the classroom (if any are available), so the exercise could be extended as a mini-survey outside class.

Timing: 20 minutes

3 Interrupting and handling interruptions

Prompt suggestions of ways to interrupt speakers in a meeting. Ask when interruptions are perhaps *not* acceptable.

Note: Different styles of interrupting apply in different situations. Appropriacy depends on place, context and the people involved. For example, internal meetings or meetings with clients, friends, status of relationships, formality, urgency, time considerations, conventions, agenda, style of discussion, etc.

Generally, the more informal the meeting, the more likely that interruptions will be acceptable. In large formal meetings, interrupting may be reserved only for the chair.

1 Use the picture to check understanding of terms like *off-road truck, four-wheel drive.* Pre-teach the term *advertising agency* and check understanding by asking what an advertising agency does. (It designs advertisements, plans campaigns, advises on where advertisements should appear, etc.)

Introduce the recording of an internal discussion in the European sales office of an American off-road automobile manufacturer, Amass. It is about advertising plans for the launch of a new truck, the Rodeo 4 PLUS.

Play the recording once. Check the True / False answers:

Key

a) True – at first.
b) False – later it will be targeted at this market as well.
c) False – he wants fresh ideas.
d) False – he used independent marketing consultants.
e) False – at most 5% more.

2 Play the recording again. Check students' answers.

Key

a) Yes, but Matt, if I can interrupt you again. We're talking serious money here. We've got to be careful … ☐7
b) Er, excuse me, Matt, just a moment. That's a big claim … ☐1
c) It's the most important thing … ☐9
d) One moment! Can we start with a few basics? ☐2
e) Yes, so, a select, professional market first, then the mass market, an on-road vehicle. ☐4
f) But why? CMA have been okay in the past. ☐6
g) Let's just clarify where … who the audience are, what's the target group? ☐3
h) What! Most agencies charge a lot more than CMA. ☐8
i) You plan to use our usual agency, CMA? ☐5

3 Allow a few minutes' discussion.

Key

The following points should be made:
a) The meeting is internal, informal but serious.
b) Matt is quite accommodating at the start, allowing many interruptions. In fact he is deflected from what he wants to say. He begins to sound defensive. Eventually he gets impatient and asks his colleagues to let him explain what the consultants have said. He actually asks them not to interrupt. This way, he hopes to regain control.
c) As for his colleagues, it seems they do not like what they hear (the change of advertising agency). They are rather impolite, making constant interruptions. They make the meeting difficult for Matt.

Timing: 20 minutes

Tapescript

PAOLO: So, Matt, the next item on the agenda is the 4 PLUS advertising campaign. Tell us about your ideas for this.

MATT: Okay. The central idea is that the Rodeo 4 PLUS is a new direction, a truck with no limits. The point is …

ROSA: Er, excuse me, Matt, just a moment. That's a big claim …

MATT: Of course it's big! This truck offers a total solution and that's …

PAOLO: One moment! Can we start with a few basics?

MATT: Sure.

PAOLO: Let's just clarify where … who the audience are, what's the target group?

MATT: Professionals, people who need a professional workhorse for a truck. Later, we go for a more mass market. That's the big idea of the 4 PLUS.

PAOLO: Yes, so, a select, professional market first, then the mass market, an on-road vehicle.

MATT: Right. Now, as I said a moment ago, I want to talk about agencies.

ROSA: You plan to use our usual agency, CMA?

MATT: Listen. We've been advised by independent consultants that we need a fresh marketing style. Our contract with CMA is almost through. We have an opportunity to take on a new agency.

ROSA: But why? CMA have been okay in the past.

MATT: We need fresh ideas, a new style. This product is different. We want to capture a specialist market and then move for a more mass market. This is new territory – a diff …

ROSA: Yes, but Matt, if I can interrupt you again. We're talking serious money here. We've got to be careful …

MATT: The costs are not going to be much higher …

PAOLO: What! Most agencies charge a lot more than CMA.

MATT: That's not true. In terms of total advertising budget. A new agency isn't going to increase our costs by more than 5%. But we can talk about costs later.

ROSA: It's the most important thing …

MATT: Rosa, listen, can I just say what I want to say? Can I say what the consultants said? Later the costs, the market, the advertising, but let me tell you … I think it's important to … it's important to understand what the experts have said. So, let me explain that first. No more interruptions …

ROSA: Okay, go on then.

MATT: Right. We've been working with a marketing consultancy with huge experience in off-road and four-wheel drive trucks.

PHOTOCOPIABLE © Cambridge University Press 2003

4 This is a controlled practice exercise.
  a) Ask students to brainstorm phrases for five different types of interruption. Possible examples are given here. Refer also to the Language Checklist.

Key
- To ask for clarification:
  Er, what exactly do you mean?
  Could you say a little more about this?
- To add opinion:
  Well, I think we should keep the same agency.
  Well, my view is …
- To ask for more details:
  Could I come in here, could you tell us about the growth forecasts?
  Do we know any more about … ?
- To change the direction of the discussion:
  Wait a moment, can we talk about … ?
  Perhaps we should discuss …
- To disagree:
  But isn't it true that … ?
  Actually, I don't think that's right …

Note: Point out that interruptions are often introduced by short expressions like *Well … , Er … , But … , Hmm … , Actually … , Yes, but … , Sorry, but … , In fact … , So … , Wait … , One moment!*

  b) Students can do this in pairs and practise the entire dialogue twice so they both use different interrupting language.
- They need to look at it for a couple of minutes first to find out which type of interruption will fit the sentence which follows.

- When they have finished, hear some students' examples, then go on to the next exercise.
- Tell students that you will play a model version of the complete dialogue shortly.

5 This exercise focuses on handling interruptions.

a) In pairs, students brainstorm phrases for the following. Possible answers are given here. Refer also to the Language Checklist.

Key

1 Promise to come back to a point later:
   If you don't mind, I'll come to that later.
   We can talk about that in a moment.

2 Politely disagree with an interruption:
   No, sorry, I cannot agree with you there.
   Well, in fact, my experience, or my understanding is different.

3 Say the interruption is not relevant or that time is short:
   Er, I think that's not absolutely relevant at the moment.
   Can we move on – I think we don't have time to go into that now.

4 Politely accept the interruption and respond to it before continuing:
   Yes, well, what I mean is …
   Certainly, this means …

5 Reject a suggestion:
   Well, no, I don't think we should.
   Not just yet.

b) Play the recording of a model version once. Students should listen for the handling of interruption phrases, matching them to the five types above. If necessary, play the extract again so they can confirm their choices.

The numbers in the brackets in the tapescript refer to the type indicated at Exercise 5a.

Tapescript

A: The fall in sales is mainly due to the recession affecting world markets.

B: *Er, can you tell us exactly how much sales have gone down?*

A: Well, it's a general fall of around 5% in sales for most product areas. Also, specifically in the oil-processing sector, we have much lower sales, mainly because we sold our UK subsidiary, Anglo Oils. (4)

B: *Can we talk about the decision to sell Anglo Oils …*

A: Well, no, I'd rather not go into that. We discussed that in previous meetings. I'd prefer to talk about future prospects. The outlook is very good just now … (3)

B: *What? I'd say things look quite bad.*

A: I'm very surprised you say that. In fact, sales forecasts are much better now. Anyway, let me tell you … (2)

B: *Sorry, I think I'd like to hear more about new markets.*

A: New markets? Yes, but can we talk about new markets later? I have some important information on that. But first … (1)

B: *Wait, don't you think we should take a short break – have a coffee?*

A: Take a break? We've only just started! (5)

6 Students should create a simple dialogue, without writing, which uses the target language of this section. If there is time, let them switch roles to practise both sides of the conversation. Listen to a few examples and give class feedback.

Timing: 30 minutes

Pronunciation option

Spend some time getting students to practise either their own versions, or to read the tapescript above (you will have to photocopy it) with special effort to vary – and to exaggerate even – the intonation and sentence stress. It could be quite entertaining, especially if you provide a somewhat exaggerated model, showing A's exasperation at the constant interruptions, or B's extreme hesitancy in interrupting. You can treat the tapescript fairly loosely to enable this to be effective.

Practice 2

Introduce the topic of public vs private transport. Divide the class into pairs and have them look at File cards 13A and 13B. Give them three minutes to prepare ideas. Student(s) B should interrupt as much as possible.

Timing: 15 minutes

Debate option

The items suggested here are big topics and can provide for up to an hour's discussion, including preparation. Alternatively, preparation could be a separate homework or self-study activity.

Subjects like these can provoke a lively classroom debate, but if you choose to include this exercise, find out first which of the options below is most popular for the group as a whole. Ask them to indicate which *two* they would most like to talk about. You then get a reasonably accurate picture of preference, though you may need a second round of voting.

Divide the class into two groups, those for and those against. There should be two leading speakers on each side. For the purposes of the debate, it is helpful if the two sides are reasonably matched in terms of numbers. If this is not possible (because everyone is of the same view) tell each group to argue either for or against the idea, *irrespective of their true feelings*.

Each team should choose a key speaker, who prepares (in note form only) a logical and coherent exposition of his / her views. If possible, speakers should support their ideas with arguments, facts and examples.

The objective is to have a reasoned discussion with the other side.

The debate should have an overall Chair to lead and control the discussion.

Here are possible topics:
1 'Murder is sometimes justifiable.'
2 'Women should stay at home and look after the family.'
3 'Private cars should be banned from the centre of cities.'
4 'Monarchies are an anachronism that should be dispensed with.'
5 'Life is more depressing now than in the pre-industrial age.'
6 'Democracy does not work.'
7 An alternative, chosen by the group.

Role play

This role play is designed to cover work from both Units 10 and 11. It requires a minimum of four participants (choose the first four roles) and a maximum of six to be effective. With a large class divide them into groups of four, five or six.

Introduce the situation by reading aloud the 'Introduction – for all participants'. Make sure all the vocabulary is understood and that the context is clear. Allow ten / fifteen minutes' preparation time. Allow 40 minutes as a maximum time for the meeting. During the meeting, monitor students' language and prepare to give ten minutes of feedback on i) the overall success of the discussion and ii) the language. Always ask students for their impression of the exercise before giving your own views. In giving language feedback, concentrate mainly on the language of chairing meetings, leading discussion, asking for and stating opinion, interrupting and handling interruptions.

There should be no need for you to intervene during the actual meeting, unless things are going seriously awry or one person is dominating.

If time is short, giving individuals written feedback could save time. However, always ensure that role play work ends with *some* comments, however short.

Timing: 15 minutes preparation, maximum 30 minutes for the meeting, maximum 15 minutes feedback.

Note: It is difficult to be prescriptive about timing for a major role play such as this. Allow ample time for preparation and allow adjournments if necessary. Help students to manage the meeting, call short breaks to offer guidance if things are not running as they should. How long you need will vary depending on the class, students' level, enthusiasm, etc.

Writing option

Possible homework or self-study activity.
Ask students to write a report on the Adel Passam Ltd. meeting.

Suggest that before they begin to write, students decide on the basic organisation of the report and what information needs to be included. Suggest that students write a brief outline before beginning the final version.

Transfer 1

This Transfer task is designed to get students to assess the Adel Passam role play meeting above. Alternatively, adapt it to suit students in work, getting them to apply the questions to work meetings.

Transfer 2

Get students to assess the decision-making strategy that may have occurred in the role play meeting, or in a real meeting that they have taken part in.

Writing option

Some students could draw up a short critical written report on the meeting and on their progress in this unit. The report could indicate:

- ways that the meeting could have been better
- comments on what they have learned from the whole unit
- reference to what they still need to do to improve their performance in meetings.

Skills Checklist

Draw attention to the DESC approach to meetings, which is especially appropriate in the case of problem-solving meetings and includes allowance for participants to express feelings about a situation, a better way to reach a full understanding and to have a good, open working relationship.

The rationale behind clearly expressing emotions and feelings is that making decisions can be easier if everyone feels that they have been able to express what they truly think. After that, they may be better able to change their minds or modify their position according to others' opinions.

Timing: 5 minutes

MODULE 4 Meetings

12 What do you mean by ... ?

AIMS	■ Asking for and giving clarification	■ Ending the meeting
	■ Delaying decisions	

Briefing

Much of the material in this unit relates closely to the next module, Negotiations. There is also a close relationship between this unit and the previous module on Presentations.

This unit contains listening extracts with a focus on functional language especially relevant to meetings. There is also a short reading text on some principles affecting how meetings should end. This includes what happens after a meeting.

The final role play offers an opportunity for a substantial meeting with fairly detailed background material. It brings together the various targets of this unit but allows one to incorporate objectives from the rest of the module.

Language and pronunciation options

There are many exponents of functional language in the recorded extracts which may be given added focus during your lessons if you think this would benefit your students. Refer also to the Language Checklist.

Again there is scope for using the listening material to focus on features of pronunciation, such as sentence stress, and intonation in question forms.

1:1 situation

All practice tasks, including the first role play, can work in the 1:1 situation. Take a role where appropriate, or guide the student through the dialogue-building exercise. The final role play could be used in a simulated meeting involving three or four 1:1 students – as suggested in the previous unit – if this is an option available to you.

Timing: 3.5 hours

1 Asking for and giving clarification

⬛◎ **1** Introduce the recording as part of a meeting about a possible site for locating a factory. The speaker, Victoria Lenning, is explaining the historical background to industry in the Basque Country in northern Spain.

Key
a) steel and paper processing
b) they have declined (but steel-related manufacturing still accounts for 44% of industrial activity)

Check these answers and elicit any other details the class can recall.

⬛◎ **2** Now focus on the two requests for clarification. Play the recording a second time, stopping it after Fred says 'Yes thanks'. Students should follow the structure and the examples given in their books. Then let the recording continue, asking students to note the equivalent phrases used in the second part.

Key
a) Sorry, Victoria. What do you mean by ... ? I'm not clear ...
b) Well, what I mean is ...
c) Is that okay? Does that make sense? ... okay?
d) Okay, right.

You could also point out the related phrases used by Victoria: *When we talk about ... , ... we'll see this in more detail, so we'll come back to this question ...*

Language focus option

Check understanding of the following words:
hinterland – the area around a major city, usually economically dependent on that city.
infrastructure – here means transport systems.
workforce – people who work or are available to work.

Tapescript

VICTORIA: ... and the main industries, the main activities in the region were historically steel – especially around the port of Bilbao – and also, er, paper processing.

FRED: Er ... sorry, can I add something? I'm not quite sure about the status of those industries now – could you tell us something about that?

VICTORIA: Yes, of course. In fact, they are less significant. But steel-related manufacturing still accounts for 44% of industrial activity, machine tools, mainly, that sort of thing, so it's still very important. In fact, 80% of Spain's machine tools are from the Basque Country. As for paper processing, yes, there's still a little, but it's no longer what it once was in the region. So ... is that clear? Okay?

FRED: Yes, thanks.

VICTORIA: Now, to get back to what I was saying. There is a lot of unemployment in the region, presently much of it in the small towns and villages that form the hinterland – in the land that forms the hinterland – to the main coastal cities of Bilbao and San Sebastian. Now, there are geographical problems, infrastructure problems in the region.

FRED: Sorry, Victoria. What do you mean by geographical problems? Or infrastructure? I'm not clear ...

VICTORIA: Well, what I mean is the area is very hilly – mountainous in parts – so there used to be transport problems. Now though, there's new train links and better roads. But it may be that some smaller towns inland remain not very well connected. Is that okay ... does that make sense? When we talk about specific location suggestions, we'll see this in more detail, so we'll come back to this question, okay?

FRED: Okay, right.

VICTORIA: So, I was about to say something about the workforce in the region and the level of training and education. In general it is very good and improving ...

Practice 1

Work through the first exchange with the whole class, then have pairs work on the other two short dialogues. To check, have pairs read their completed dialogues. Play the model answers on the tape. Get students to identify any differences and / or suggest alternatives.

Tapescript

Extract 1

A: Brunei has a tropical climate.

B: Excuse me, *what do you mean* by 'tropical'?

A: *Well*, it's hot almost all the year, with heavy rainfall in the rainy season. *Okay*?

B: *Right*, I understand.

Extract 2

A: Every new product needs a USP.

B: *Excuse me, what's* USP?

A: Unique Selling Proposition.

B: Er, can you *explain* what that is?

A: USP *means* the special characteristics of a product which make it different and desirable – so consumers will want it. Er, *is* that *clear* now?

B: Yes, *I understand now*. Thanks.

Timing: 40 minutes

2 Delaying decisions

Elicit examples of sentences used to delay decisions. Offer as an example *We don't have enough information on this yet* or *We cannot take any action until the report is completed*. Write these on the board or on a flip chart. Encourage students to copy them down.

📼 ◎ **1** Introduce the recording, explaining that it is a continuation of the discussion about the Basque Country.

Check comprehension of the words on the flip chart in the drawing. Together they explain the meaning of *infrastructure*. A *dry port* is a point to and from which containers are moved by land. They are often directly linked to *sea ports* to facilitate rapid transport of goods.

Play the extract once and check these answers:

Key

   a) mostly good
   b) Bilbao
   c) a fast train link
   d) made bigger

Elicit any other information students understood on first listening.

2 In pairs, get students to compare their suggestions for how to complete the sentences. Elicit ideas, praising good ones but indicating if any are incorrect. Then play the recording again so they can compare their suggestions against the actual phrases on the recording. Finally, ask for more suggestions for possible alternatives.

Key

On the recording are the following:
   a) Well, let's not *rush into anything*. I think …
   b) It *might be better* to think about …
   c) Yes, we could do that, but we *need*, I think, *first, to check* a few things. For example …
   d) … but also, *one moment*.
   e) So *I don't think we can decide* at this stage.

Pronunciation option

Play the part of the recording where John says 'one moment'. The pause which follows has the effect of giving him full control and everyone's attention. It gives more emphasis to what he has to say.

Tapescript

VICTORIA: So, possible locations for the plant. First, the infrastructure for the region is generally very good, at least between the three main cities, Bilbao, Vitoria in the south – and San Sebastian. There is now a fast train link to the south of France – and to the rest of Spain. Other improvements affect Bilbao, principally, but the whole region benefits. First, the port area has been completely modernised and relocated and the airport has also been extended. So, infra-structure is good.

FRED: Right, so are we in a position to choose one of these cities?

VICTORIA: Well, let's not rush into anything. I think it would be a bad idea to assume we're going to choose a city. It might be better to think about one of the smaller towns.

FRED: … smaller places, yes. So, should we get details on these possible places?

VICTORIA: Yes, we could do that, but we need, I think, first, to check a few things. For example, tax benefits, grants and anything like that – for locating to a smaller place, not one of the main cities. Then we could make a better decision.

JOHN: Yes, I agree, but also, one moment. … er … you've talked about the improved transport links, the trains, the airport, the port in Bilbao. What about the links, to these er … the smaller towns? If it's a mountainous or hilly region, it could take an hour – or more – for a truck to reach a main road. So I don't think we can decide at this stage. I think we need to look specifically at the train and road links for smaller towns …

VICTORIA: Yes, you're right – road and rail – and the financial position. In fact, I have some – a bit on the transport question, because … last month …

Practice 2

This is designed to get students to use the language studied in this section:

- Do the first example with the whole class, then students work in pairs.
- Get them to switch roles so they practise both sides of the dialogue.
- They should not need to write anything.
- Ask a selection of pairs to perform dialogues.
- Finally, play the recording of a model version and compare it to students' versions.

1:1 situation

Perform the exercise twice, so the student plays both roles.

Timing: 40 minutes

Tapescript

A: Can we reach a decision on this?

B: Well, I … I think … er, I think we need more information.

A: Hmm. Can you explain – say exactly what sort of detail you think we need?

B: Well, I feel first of all, we need to know more about the effects of a price increase.

A: Perhaps we should, er, commission some market research?

B: Yes, I agree. That's right. We could ask Hamid to recommend someone.

A: Well, I think before that we could look at our own experience of price rises. Then later we can perhaps ask a marketing consultancy. Does everyone agree with that proposal?

ALL: (*murmurs of agreement*)

A: Okay, let's move to the next item on the agenda.

3 Ending the meeting

With reference to the cartoon, ask students what they think should happen at the end of a meeting.

- Tell them to think about the role of the chair.
- Elicit comments on the problem in the meeting shown. Focus especially on the chair: smug, disinterested, he has his own agenda.

Then ask students:

- what should happen *after* a meeting?
- if they have any suggestions on ways to improve meetings.

If the two questions above – and your prompting – are unproductive, say that there are suggestions in the following text.

1 Introduce the text from a management training book. Ask students to read it and to identify *a* and *b*.

Note: Note-taking is not necessary. Students need only pick out the relevant phrases from the text.

Key

   a) • a restatement of objectives
      • a summary of what has been accomplished (elicit comment on what this means)
      • a summary of what action must be taken after the meeting.
   b) Meetings should be part of a learning experience, so future meetings can be improved by asking participants to evaluate meetings.

Add a further suggestion for what should happen after a meeting (not included in the reading text):

- the main decisions should be circulated in a memorandum. This should be sent to all participants and anyone interested, but unable to attend.

2 Explain that you are going to play a recording of the end of the meeting about locating a factory in the Basque Country.

a) Before you play it, ask the whole class to recap the *main points* from the previous two extracts:

- good location, good telecommunications and transport infrastructure, skilled workforce
- need for more information on costs, financial assistance, especially affecting choice between cities or small towns.

Get the whole class to predict what the end of the meeting will include. Prompt them by asking if it will *only* include a summary. Students may refer to Haynes's suggestions.

b) Ask students to read the three summaries in their book, then play the tape. Students say which is the best summary, A, B or C. They may be critical and say that even B is not totally adequate.

Key
B

3 If necessary, play the recording again. In fact, the meeting ends without meeting several of Haynes's recommendations:

Key

- there is no clear restatement of objectives
- there *is* a summary of what has been accomplished, but is it sufficient?
- there is no summary of what action must be taken *after* the meeting, no one's specific responsibilities are stated
- no written report is referred to
- it is not obvious that there will be any formal evaluation of the meeting.

Students might also suggest that no date is fixed for a follow-up meeting.

Tapescript

JOHN: So I think that's about as far as we can go, isn't it, Vict ... ?

VICTORIA: ... Yes, I think so, unless there are any more questions?

JOHN: No, I think we're through at that. Fred?

FRED: Okay.

JOHN: So, can you summarise, Victoria?

VICTORIA: Yes, well, we've discussed the Spanish Basque Country as a possible site for locating a new plant. The area looks a good long-term prospect and there is a high quality transport infrastructure and telecommunications systems – also excellent. The one thing we have to make more enquiries about, to find out more about, is the financial aspect relating to choosing a city location – or a small town location. So ... that's all.

FRED: Good. That's it then?

JOHN: Okay, thanks for coming. Oh Fred, can I have a word about something else ... er ... thanks.

VICTORIA: I'll see you later.

Practice 3

This exercise can be done in pairs, without writing. Encourage students to use their imaginations to add realistic detail. Play the recording of a model answer at the end. Students can compare this with their own versions.

Writing option

As a written option, it could be a self-study or homework exercise.

Tapescript

SPEAKER: So, we've almost finished. Does anyone have anything else to say? Well, we had to decide on action regarding training courses. To summarise, to confirm our decision, we've agreed a £10,000 budget. And also that Peter is going to identify three possible training organisations. Is everyone happy? Is that okay? Now, Peter will organise a presentation for next week, on the 14th at 2 p.m. Until then, thanks everyone for coming. That's it for today.

Practice 4

Remind students that for this exercise, the recording they have just heard for Practice 3 can serve as a model.

Discuss all four options first, checking that the vocabulary is understood. Have students choose which they want to work on, or you divide them into four groups, A–D, of roughly equal numbers. After five minutes' working together to check the language required and add any other information they need, set up different groups of one each from A–D. They then present their closing remarks in these new groups and give each other feedback.

Timing: 40 minutes

Role play

Have the class work in groups of three or four. In a group of three, leave out File card 33, or combine the information there with File card 32. If your class has only two students, you could take one of the roles in File cards 30–33.

Begin by having the class read the flyer for Sola Holidays. Check understanding. Then get each group to decide roles and read their individual file cards. They then read the background information and the agenda. Check for any difficulties.

The role of the chair is crucial. Let students in each group decide who takes this role. During the preparation time, remind the Chair(s) to begin the meeting, introduce the agenda, the objective for the meeting and to make the opening statement covering the background. Clearly final decisions cannot be made at this meeting, so the meeting should end with a summary of what has been agreed and the next steps.

Allow no more than 10–15 minutes'

preparation. Remind students to use language practised in this unit, and in the two preceding ones. Suggest looking at the Language and Skills Checklists. The meeting should last 20–30 minutes.

You may:
- choose to audio- or video- record the meeting.
- take notes to help with feedback.

You should:
- note good use of target language, good conduct of the meeting(s) and how the meeting was controlled by the Chair.

Fifth person option

If there are sufficient students, include a role for a secretary to take the minutes and read them out at the end of the meeting.

Or, have a fifth person assume another identity and have similar views to one of the existing File cards. He / She can improvise additional points.

Video recording

Use of a video to record the meeting can usefully introduce a degree of extra pressure on students' performances. It can also give an opportunity for individuals to review their own performance in more detail after class. If you choose to look at the video as part of feedback in class, take care not to dwell on negative aspects or spend too long on any single individual. In any case, keep reviewing down to a minimum of ten minutes for a 20-minute meeting – so use fast forward and give everyone equal playback time. Elicit students' comments on what they see and hear.

1:1 option

Adapt the role play to a discussion between just two people, yourself and the student. The student can take the role of Managing Director and Chair, you are the Marketing Director. The information on the other two File cards can be added to those for the Chair and the Marketing Director.

Depending on circumstances, you may be able to pool different students on 1:1 courses in a simulated meeting using this material.

Timing: 1 hour

Transfer

Once again, students should evaluate the meeting they have taken part in and may produce a short summary of their impressions of the good and less good aspects of the meeting. They can refer in particular to their own roles or their own contributions.

This can be extended to an evaluation of the unit as a whole, including reference to areas where special care is needed to achieve further improvement. Finally, students may reflect on the entire Meetings module.

Option

Have students think about a real meeting they have attended recently. How did it end? Did it meet the recommendations made in this unit and in the Skills Checklist?

Skills Checklist

Refer for the final time to the points included in the Checklist, including how the Chair should end the meeting and what should happen after a meeting. The point about a memorandum is especially important here.

The section on how to improve meetings may generate a little more discussion on the usefulness of evaluation methods for internal meetings.

Timing: 10 minutes

13 Know what you want

AIMS	■ Types of negotiation	■ Making an opening statement
	■ Preparation for a negotiation	

Briefing

While it is possible to use the Negotiations module on its own, there is no doubt that intermediate-level students would benefit from studying the Meetings module first, as the language burden in the recorded extracts in this final module is slightly higher, especially in Units 14 and 15. This is perhaps inevitable in dealing with areas like bargaining and making concessions (see Unit 14). Students who have studied other modules will also be more used to the skills-driven approach used in this course.

The unit begins by looking at different types of negotiation, then draws on students' thoughts on preparation for negotiations, before offering some recommendations to help develop effective negotiating skills.

The importance of the opening statement in a formal negotiation echoes the role of the introduction in a presentation (see Unit 6). The unit includes an example of an opening statement before giving students practice in this area.

The role play which follows is an opportunity to practise both the preparation for a negotiating situation and an opening statement. The role play is actually developed in the optional Case Study 1. This can be used either after Unit 14, or at the end of the course. Units 14 and 15 look at the development of negotiations after the opening statements.

The Skills Checklist in this unit is especially important and should be seen as integral to the section on Preparation for a negotiation.

1:1 situation

The unit presents no special complications, just the usual need for extra guidance and prompting from you. The issues raised in the unit are sometimes complex. Your support will be required, especially since students do not have the advantage of having ideas triggered by other group members. That said, more experienced students are likely to be quite forthcoming with ideas.

Timing: 3 hours

1 Types of negotiation

Spend a few minutes on the meaning of the term *negotiation*. Elicit ideas for a definition. Students may focus on negotiations in a professional or business context, but point out that negotiations happen in many other contexts. Students' suggestions need to include concepts such as the existence of two or more parties, specified goals, discussion, compromise and agreement. A fairly all-inclusive definition, which you may suggest, is 'a conversation between two parties to reach agreement on future action', but you will have your own ideas.

1 Introduce the recording of a conversation between two friends. Play it twice. Ask students to identify:
- the first suggestion (film)
- the counter-suggestion (go out for a meal with two friends, Mary and Thomas)
- the final agreement (to go out with them).

Tapescript

JACK: What shall we do on Saturday?

JILL: Er … let's go and see a film.

JACK: We could do that – or what if … you know it's Mary's birthday? Why don't we go out with her and Thomas – go for a meal or something?

JILL: That's a good idea – where shall we go?

2 Elicit comment on the similarities between ordinary conversations like this and business negotiations. Students may suggest that the typical structure shown in their book reflects the structure of the conversation between two friends that they have just heard, except that there was no confirmation. Ask students to suggest how this conversation could develop. It could in fact lead to a confirmation, such as 'Right, then. I'll phone Thomas and see what he says to that idea', i.e. to go to a particular restaurant.

Get pairs of students to suggest a business conversation with the given structure. If necessary, give the suggestion *What about a 10% discount for immediate payment?* Hear students' versions and / or offer this model:

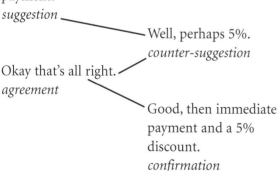

What about a 10% discount for immediate payment?
suggestion

Well, perhaps 5%.
counter-suggestion

Okay that's all right.
agreement

Good, then immediate payment and a 5% discount.
confirmation

In conclusion, confirm that the structure of the conversation on the tape between two friends and the structure of business negotiations is often similar.

🔊 ◎ 3

a) Check that the task is clear. Introduce the recording: explain that it contains three short extracts from different types of negotiation. Play all three extracts once. Students match the extracts and pictures.

Key

Extract 1, Picture C.

Extract 2, Picture A.

Extract 3, Picture B.

Tapescript

Extract 1

LAWYER: Yes, I understand what you are saying, but the facts are clear. The company was responsible for carrying out all the safety checks. Those checks were not made.

MANAGER: That's what you say …

LAWYER: There is evidence that safety practices were poor. You know that. I advise you to make a settlement, Mr Cooper. If not, I think it could be worse for the company. You don't want the press involved in this.

Extract 2

FIRST MAN: The price includes all the land and the buildings.

SECOND MAN: Yes. What about the payment terms? With better terms, you could accept a lower price?

FIRST MAN: No, I think terms are not the problem. The issue is price, Mr Ford. We have had several offers.

Extract 3

WOMAN: Yes, what looks good here is the practical qualities of the building and the use of natural materials, stone, glass, wood. It's very attractive.

ARCHITECT: I thought you'd like it. But we'd like to discuss some other possibilities, though. There are different options – we need to get things right – absolutely right.

WOMAN: Yes, we need to talk about the time schedule, too.

b) Play the recording again. Students match each extract with the correct description.

Key

Extract 1, Picture C, Description Z.
Extract 2, Picture A, Description Y.
Extract 3, Picture B, Description X.

Discussion

Briefly elicit examples of different negotiating situations, seeking to consolidate understanding of the three types of negotiation. Ask students to think about their own personal experiences of negotiating. Examples could include:

- Agreement-based:
  - employment contracts
  - tenancy agreements
  - service relationships.
- Independent advantage:
  - private sales
  - hard-selling (home improvements)
  - looking for a discount on the asking price for goods
  - in shops.
- Win / lose:
  - compensation
  - custody battles
  - warranty disputes.

Timing: 30 minutes

2   Preparation for a negotiation

Remind students that everyone has *some* experience of negotiating. Ask them to think what preparation for a negotiation should include and what considerations a negotiator has to make before negotiating. Prepare suggestions in pairs first. Brainstorm ideas, putting them on a board or OHT.

1 Introduce the recording. Diana Ferry, a Management Communications Consultant, talks about preparing for a negotiation. Play it once. Check the order of the seven points mentioned.

Key

Identify your minimum requirements. [2]
Prepare your opening statement. [7]
Decide what concessions you could make. [3]
Know your own strengths and weaknesses. [4]
Know your role as part of a team. [6]
Prepare your negotiating position – know your aims and objectives. [1]
Prepare any figures, any calculations and any support materials you may need. [5]

2   Students may be able to do this without listening a second time to the recording. However, play it a second time so they can check their answers.

Key

a) ii)
b) iv)
c) i)
d) iii)

Tapescript

SPEAKER: I think first of all ... I would have to say that one needs to be very ... er prepared ... I mean to know what you want from a negotiation, what's your purpose, your aims and objectives. Without clear aims, you can't have clear thinking, so aims are vital, to have a clear purpose. What do you want? A contract? You want a firm agreement – or just to find out a few things?

Then, you ... you have to know what's the minimum deal. Decide what is the least – the lowest offer you can accept for a deal – an agreement.

Then you have to know where you can give way – or make concessions. So fixing concessions – and targets – is important. Without that you end up agreeing to something and later thinking 'Oh no that's a bad deal!' – or you miss out on what *seemed* a bad deal at the time but was in fact ... okay – not bad anyway.

Another area – perhaps obvious – is to know your strengths and your weaknesses. If we take the classic marketing SWOT analysis – you have to understand your own strengths and weaknesses as well as the opportunities and threats – or dangers – that exist outside, from competitors for example. So, know the market, know your strengths, know about prices and other possibilities. If you do this, you can see the negotiation in its proper context.

Then you need to prepare all support information. Figures, numbers, pictures, whatever. It could be anything – but the most important thing is that you can support what you say. It helps you to be clear.

Next, the team has to be well prepared, well managed. If … if it's a team you have, everyone needs a clear role, clear responsibilities – to have roles.

Finally, your opening remarks. Prepare what to say. Begin in general terms what you hope to achieve – the general intention, what you're looking for. The opening statement sets up the right atmosphere, the right expectations, it helps things to be clear between the two sides.

PHOTOCOPIABLE   © Cambridge University Press 2003

Refer again to students' suggestions for what the preparation for a negotiation should involve. Then refer to the Skills Checklist on page 130 which is fairly comprehensive. Explain the Checklist, beginning with the seven key areas, then going through each of them. Start with *Type of negotiation.*

Timing: 25 minutes

Practice 1

1   Discuss the cartoon. Check that students understand it. Check understanding of words like *commission* and *sales representative.*

- Ask the class to suggest how the negotiation in the cartoon could have reached a more satisfactory conclusion.
- Have the whole class brainstorm ideas on what each side would need to think about to prepare for a meeting between a sales manager and a sales rep who wanted a pay rise. Suggestions could include:

Sales manager
- sales results
- pictures
- comparison with other years
- market trends
- company finances

Sales representative
- estimate of improved performance
- comparison with pay in other companies
- evidence of low morale among staff

2   After a maximum of five minutes, divide the class into As and Bs. They read the corresponding note in their books, then in groups of up to four, they prepare for the meeting. They need to decide what they are going to say. Allow a short preparation. Have the class then regroup in pairs, or with a large class in groups of four, two sales managers negotiating with two sales reps. After five minutes, get feedback on the results from each negotiation. Give some language feedback too, but treat the exercise as a fluency practice. More detailed language work is provided in the next two units.

1:1 situation

With a 1:1 class, you take one of the roles. Then switch over so the student practises both sides of the situation.

Timing: 20 minutes

3 Making an opening statement

Introduce the idea of an opening statement, already referred to in the recording for Section 2, Exercise 1, about preparing for a negotiation. Elicit ideas on what an opening statement should include.

Key

Welcome / Pleased to be here, agenda, statement of main objectives, expectations, optimistic look ahead to reaching agreement, timetable. The most important points are the welcome / pleased to be here and the statement of objectives.

🔲◉ **1** Introduce the recording of part of the LP Associates / Kee Ltd. joint venture negotiation. Play it twice. Students should identify four broad objectives of the negotiation:

LP Associates want to reach a final agreement in this negotiation. ☐
These are preliminary talks. ☑
The two parties want to resolve a conflict. ☐
They want to agree on a name for the joint venture. ☐
LP Associates would like to consider joint product development. ☑
They would also consider licence agreements. ☑
LP Associates want to agree a complete sale of their ideas. ☐
They want to consider working on a consultancy basis. ☑

🔲◉ **2** Play the recording again, explaining that students should focus specifically on the language used. Ask students to complete the given phrases.

Key

a) Well, thank you *for coming here today.*
b) May I begin by *outlining some basic thoughts* ...
c) First of all, we see it very much as a first meeting, a *preliminary negotiation* to *identify ways* in which we can *perhaps* ...
d) There are two, possibly three, ways in which we *might go forward.*
e) I'd like to *summarise* these under three headings.

3 Have the class compare what Stella Wang says with their own suggestions for what should be in an opening statement. Help students identify points which she makes which match their suggestions, and any additional points.

Key

She:

- thanks the other party for coming
- explains the purpose of the meeting – a preliminary negotiation to identify possible ways to work together (goals)
- explains specific areas that they can discuss (sets a form of agenda).

Tapescript

Well, thank you for coming here today. As you know, we have a busy agenda. May I begin by outlining some basic thoughts that we have on this meeting. First of all, we see it very much as a first meeting, a preliminary negotiation to identify areas in which we can perhaps work together on certain products – prototype products – that we have developed. There are two, possibly three, ways in which we might go forward. I'd like to summarise these under three headings. First, development projects, second, licence agreements. The third is the possibility of some kind of consultancy relationship. Is everyone happy if I say a few words about these to begin with? (*murmurs of agreement*) Right, well, first of all, joint development projects. This is ...

Timing: 25 minutes

Practice 2

1 This exercise can be done in open class, eliciting various suggestions from different students. Alternatively, they can work in pairs. It is intended as a brief step towards the freer practice that follows. Another option is to set it as a homework or a self-study option. Refer to the Language Checklist.

The key here gives only a few suggestions. Many others are possible.

Key

a) Well, welcome to ... It's very good that you could come to see us here.
b) I hope you had a good trip? Not too long ... ? Did you get a taxi when you arrived here?

c) At lunchtime we'll be able to show you a little bit of the city – have something to eat in a local restaurant.

d) Well, shall we make a start?

e) Okay, well, can I ask Luke Fox, from our Marketing Department, to begin our discussions with some opening remarks. I think you've met James already this morning, and a little while ago too?

f) Firstly, we see this meeting as an exploratory session, I think it's best for both of us that we look at some general questions.

g) We'd like to establish the beginnings of a partnership … It would be particularly interesting for us to learn about your supply systems … about price variations and about supply costs.

2 Encourage various individuals to present answers to a–g as a single speech. For this to work effectively as a fluency exercise they should not read any more than the basic prompts given in the Student's Book (i.e. not read their own prepared notes on the various phrases).

Timing: 20 minutes

Practice 3

Students should spend five minutes preparing an opening statement for one of the given situations. It will probably work best if the class divide equally between Situations 1 and 2, then present to a partner who has chosen the other topic. Listen to various pairs practising and choose two or three individuals to repeat their opening statements for the whole group.

Check understanding of the vocabulary in the two situations.

Timing: 20 minutes

Role play

Make clear the three purposes of the role play:
- to practise preparing for a negotiation
- to prepare an opening statements as a team
- to have one or two people in each team

present the opening statement.

Divide the class into teams of up to four people, Team(s) A (File card 14A) and Teams(s) B (File card 14B).

If you only have two students, then they can each represent one of the two companies. In a class of eight, stick with just two teams. With more than eight, make teams of two, three or four.

Remind the class to think about how to establish a good working relationship with the other side at the very beginning of the negotiation: small talk and eventually a clear opening statement.

Once roles have been decided, explain that:
- the meeting is in Italy
- the supplier is Coen Brothers, an Anglo-Dutch provider of prefabricated buildings
- Coen Brothers supply complete building, materials and construction
- the purchaser is Fratelli Taviani, an Italian agricultural feeds merchant.

Note: The negotiation itself is developed in the optional Case Study 1. This can be done after Unit 14 or at the end of the course.

Monitor the group work on the preparation, prompting and making constructive comments. Get them to refer to the Skills Checklist as well as the File cards. After ten minutes' preparation, each group should be ready to talk to you about their preparation, to explain their thoughts and ideas and to describe their plans for the negotiation. This should be to you only and not for the benefit of the other party. They should briefly summarise what they want to say in the opening statement. Once you have checked this planning phase and made any further suggestions, then you can call the groups together for their meeting and each team presents its opening statement.

You may video-record the actual start of the negotiation. Elicit students' own comments on their group performance and the performance of others and you should also add selective positive and constructive / critical feedback.

1:1 situation

There are two options. Either the student concentrates on just one company and prepares that role, while you prepare the other, or the student can treat each role as a case study and prepare both roles, leading to an opening statement for each one. Later, if you use Case Study 1 in which the negotiation is developed, you can take one of the team roles.

Timing: 30 minutes

Transfer

There are two alternatives here; the first is more targeted at students who are in work. It can be an optional homework activity, in which students make notes to answer the questions or simply tell you – and the class – about their own negotiating experiences.

The second option is perhaps more oriented towards pre-service students. It asks them to consider a negotiating situation in their private (non-business) lives. Again, it is an opportunity for students to refer in a general sense to their own real experiences of negotiating.

Note: There is a third alternative. Ask students to apply these questions to their preparation for the role play they have begun above.

14 Getting what you can

AIMS

- Bargaining and making concessions
- Accepting and confirming
- Summarising and looking ahead

Briefing

This unit opens with a reading text containing specific advice on negotiating technique. It goes on to examine in some detail key language functions in effective negotiating. There are five recorded extracts which illustrate some of these techniques and offer examples of language used in negotiating.

While the recordings are quite challenging – more difficult than in previous units – the tasks that accompany them are designed to make them accessible. Some pre-teaching of terms and a clearly established context will help. As usual, students are encouraged to listen globally and to understand the main points before focusing on target language.

Four practice tasks and one or two short role plays are included. These provide preparation for performing the first of the two optional Case Studies at the end of the book. The first one is a role play which builds on the situation established in Unit 13. You and your students may prefer to postpone looking at this Case Study until after the final unit, Unit 15.

Estimating the timing of this unit will depend very largely on how much time the role play negotiations take. Allow extra time for these if they are working especially well.

1:1 situation

With more opportunity for individual attention, the 1:1 can spend more time in class on hearing recordings of practice tasks. Try to develop effective self-assessment strategies, which means noticing what is good as well as what needs

improvement. Spotting language mistakes and suggesting better alternatives is a key skill in building improved accuracy and better overall language competence.

Try to prompt discussion, drawing on the student's own experience, both in a professional and in a pre-service or private capacity. Remember, everyone has experience of negotiating to some extent. Refer to the previous unit which identified similarities between professional negotiating and negotiating in one's private, social life.

Timing: 3 hours

1 Bargaining and making concessions

The cartoon illustrates the principle contained in the opening quotation, though clearly participants need to listen, hear and respond to what the other side suggests. The illustration also shows another key principle, that of linking together different aspects in the negotiation, or treating the whole as a package.

1 Introduce the reading text with the usual advice to students that they should not read the text in detail, but should merely look for key ideas to respond to the True / False exercise. They may read the statements first and try to predict what the text will say. They should then read the text in three or four minutes to confirm their predictions.

The answers to the True / False exercise are given here:

a) T

b) F Better not to guess (though privately you might to some extent).

c) T

d) F Issues are best dealt together with other issues, in a package.

e) T One should usually be prepared to make concessions.

f) T

g) F No, one can keep on talking and find a way round the problem.

2 Have students read the text a second time, again for only three or four minutes. They may check answers in pairs.

Key

a) Check what they say without commenting, at least not immediately.

b) Vary the quantity or the quality, or bring in third parties.

c) Be prepared, think about the whole package, be constructive.

Check understanding of all these points and invite questions on vocabulary in the text.

▣ ◎ **3** Introduce the recording of the Arco / CAS negotiation. Make sure the background is clear. Provoke a short discussion on what happens when someone breaks a contract or backs out of a joint venture. Explain the words *compensation* and *the reversal of rights*. Explain the latter as follows:

Jill invents a product.

She makes an agreement with Jack to share profits from the product if Jack will promote it.

Jack later wants to back out of the contract.

Jill at this point will want all future rights (to profits) to revert to her. (If Jack is not in the partnership, then he gets no profits.)

Key

a) True

b) True

c) False: It will not be difficult.

▣ ◎ **4** Play the recording again. Ask students to identify the language used to link issues in this extract.

Key

a) We want compensation to *take* our work *into account*.

b) Yes, we *can agree* to that, *so long as* we can accept your compensation demands.

c) So, we need to *link* the question of rights to compensation.

d) The problem is that *if we* revert all rights, we *have to* keep the compensation within *acceptable limits*.

Timing: 30 minutes

Tapescript

CELIA: One consideration is the question of compensation to CAS, another is the reversal of all rights presently held by Arco. Now, clearly the question of rights is very important to us.

DIETMAR: Yes, yes, we understand that. But, we have to think about the joint development aspects. The fuel injection system has been developed using Arco technical expertise. In fact, we are happy that you have all the rights, we accept that the engine is basically your design. On the other hand, since we have contributed to the engine, we hope that the compensation we agree to pay … we want compensation to take our work into account.

CELIA: So you're prepared to give up all rights, basically the whole product reverts to CAS?

DIETMAR: Yes, we can agree to that … so long as we can accept your compensation demands. So, we need to link the question of rights to compensation.

CELIA: Well, as you know, we've been thinking about compensation based on two years' earnings from the product.

DIETMAR: Right, I think Erich has some comments on the two years' proposal.

ERICH: Yes, we feel that two years is a little too long, especially if we revert all rights to CAS. The problem is that if we revert all rights, we have to keep the compensation within acceptable limits. Two years is a lot. We believe this, particularly because you *will* find a *new* partner. And this is important: the time spent this year has included useful advances, good progress, in the design. So we need you to reduce your compensation demands a bit.

Practice 1

This exercise can be done orally in class, taking different alternative suggestions from different individuals, or in pairs, or reserved for homework or self-study and checked in class later. Here are model answers:

Key

b) We can give you free delivery with a larger order.

c) We provide free on-site training for only a small price increase.

d) We can give you a 5% discount if you agree to payment on delivery.

e) We can offer you an extra £50,000 compensation in exchange for your agreement not to go to law.

f) We promise to improve safety for staff provided that we reach agreement on new contracts.

g) The company will introduce better working conditions if the staff accept shorter breaks.

Timing: 10 minutes

Practice 2

Students should work in pairs. Get them to choose an item to negotiate over. First, they should spend three minutes preparing, then commence negotiating. Remind them to link issues – to negotiate on a broad front, thinking of 'the package'.

They should include an opening statement and they must reach agreement.

Timing: 15 minutes

2 Accepting and confirming

1   Recap on what the first extract contained: discussion on compensation to CAS and the reversal of rights to CAS. In principle Arco agree to this, but point out that they have contributed to developing the engine.

After confirming the above, introduce another stage from the same negotiation. Explain that the two parties are discussing compensation for CAS and a royalty payment to Arco. Remind students that the royalty is to take into account Arco contributions to the development of the engine.

You will probably need to play the recording twice. Make sure students understand the two pieces of information they are listening for.

Key

a) CAS are a small company, they need the money, they have spent a year on this joint venture. Now they have to find a new partner.

b) Compensation based on profit on sales over two years, and Arco would have a 10% royalty on profits from eventual production.

▭◎ 2   Explain that this task requires detailed listening for language. Play the recording again. Ask students to get you to stop the recording when they identify the relevant phrases. Use rewind as required, so they can write in the missing words.

Key

a) can agree

b) if you can settle on, we'll accept

c) we can agree to linked to

d) confirm that, in principle

At the end of this section, point out how the language students have studied, and the recording they have heard, also illustrate the principles expressed in the first section of this unit: that issues under negotiation are usually looked at together, not in isolation. In this case, it is compensation and the royalty agreement.

Timing: 25 minutes

Tapescript

CELIA: So, we need to link the royalty to the compensation. Can we suggest a 5% royalty and a compensation based on two years?

ERICH: I think the royalty is too low.

CELIA: Okay, I think we could give a little there … how about a 7.5% royalty, but keeping the two-year compensation?

DIETMAR: Can I ask why this two-year figure is so important?

CELIA: Well, we're obviously dependent on selling our projects. We're a small company, we need to see our products developed. In this case, we've seen a year's work come to a sudden end with no production in sight. Of course, we hope to find another partner – I think we will – but it'll take time, so in the meantime we need income. That's why good compensation is important to us. We can agree to a royalty, because once we're paying a royalty, we've got an income to support it.

DIETMAR: Yes, I see that. Well, if you can settle on a 10% royalty, we'll accept that – the two years' compensation.

CELIA: Okay, in principle we can agree to 10% – linked to compensation based on two years' projected sales. These details might be affected by the actual destiny of the product – I mean supposing we sold it outright, then we'd have to reach a different settlement, but we can discuss that later. I think we have to keep that option open …

ERICH: Yes, okay. So, confirmation, to confirm that, in principle we are agreeing … we agree a two-year sales forecast compensation – less costs of course – so it's profit on sales?

CELIA: Yes, of course, we understand that.

ERICH: And Arco would have a 10% royalty on profits from eventual production, subject to some other kind of deal that you might have with a third party.

We'd have to look at any agreement you eventually come up with.

Practice 3

Introduce the situation, explain any words or content in the flow chart which is not clear. Students should work in pairs, or in a large class in groups of four, where each side in the dialogue is represented by a pair who support each other.

Monitor students' efforts and hear dialogues from various pairs. Elicit feedback and comment from the group. Give some yourself.
Finally play the recording of a model version. Check understanding.

Tapescript

OJANPERA: Well, we're happy to buy a machine if you can give us a good price.

BECK: I'm sure we can. As you know our prices are very competitive.

OJANPERA: Even so, I'm sure you can allow us a discount?

BECK: Okay, well a discount could be possible if you agree to pay for the shipping costs.

OJANPERA: That sounds okay, if the discount is a good one.

BECK: How about 4%?

OJANPERA: 6% would be better.

BECK: I'm sorry, we can't manage that unless you pay for the installation.

OJANPERA: Okay, our engineers will take care of that.

BECK: Okay then, so to confirm: a 6% discount but you pay all the shipping and installation costs.

OJANPERA: That sounds all right.

Timing: 15 minutes

Language focus option

☰◉ Play the recording with frequent pauses after each contribution, following the flow chart. Get students to pick out more or less exactly what is said.

Note in particular where issues are linked.

3 Summarising and looking ahead

1 Initiate a short discussion on what 'Summarising and looking ahead' probably involves in terms of content and language. Then introduce the recording of the end of a negotiation between Gibson Trust Ltd. and government officials responsible for the sale of a former railway station. As usual, check that students fully understand the context of the recording.

a) Play the recording and have students label the plan as shown in the key below.

Key

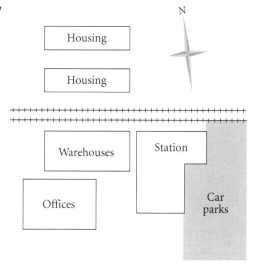

b) The housing on the north side of the railway lines is not included in the sale.
c) May 15 – meeting to examine development plans.
   September – sign contracts.

2 Play the recording again.

Key

a) She says: Well, *I'd like to summarise* – go over the *points we've agreed* on. Is that okay? …
   … Well *the first point* is …

Play the opening remarks from Jill Kearne again if necessary, to confirm the target language in a) above.
b) Positive and constructive.

Tapescript

JILL: Well, I'd like to summarise – go over the points we've agreed on. Is that okay?

NEIL: Yes, of course, go ahead.

JILL: Well, the first point is that the property includes all the land presently occupied by the station buildings and also the former car parks to the east of the station, the offices here to the west and the warehouses alongside the tracks. It does not include the present government-owned housing on the north side of the old railway lines. We also agree that the station will be renovated by the Transport Department and turned into a museum. The government will be responsible for running the eventual museum and paying a rent of £100,000 per year to Gibson Trust. The remaining land will be developed by Gibson Trust and later sold off separately. Is that an accurate summary?

NEIL: Yes, that's right, it's fine.

JILL: Okay. So, I think that's fine, then. Shall we stop there? I think we've gone as far as we can today. We just need to decide on our next meeting. Can we do that now? I mean sort out the next steps …

NEIL: Yes, okay …

JILL: Well, as I understand it, in our next meeting we should examine development plans. Finally, we'll draw up contracts. Then we'll need a little while to consider the contracts. So, probably everything should be in place for signing contracts by the end of September. Does that sound reasonable?

NEIL: Yes, September, that should be okay. So when can we meet to look at development plans?

JILL: Er, could it be May 15? Or any time that week?

NEIL: May 15 would be okay, same time? 10 a.m.?

JILL: Yes, that's okay, well, thanks for coming then, and I'm glad we've been able to make progress, to reach agreement, you know, it's been very constructive, and of course we'll send you a report.

3 Preferably a homework or self-study task. Below is the complete letter, which you may choose to copy and give out as a model.

Key

a) confirm   f) developed
b) agreed   g) specified
c) enclosed   h) examined
d) included   i) drawn up
e) excluded   j) signed

Timing: 25 minutes

Practice 4

Check understanding of both the situation and the task. Have students do this individually.

Confident students can perhaps manage the task with virtually no preparation. Others will need three or four minutes to collect their ideas and practise it – perhaps in pairs. Hear some examples and elicit / give feedback.

▱ ◉ Finally, you can play the recording of a model version.

Tapescript

SPEAKER: So, as we've covered the agenda, this is perhaps a good time to summarise what we've agreed. We began by discussing the plans for the station renovation and use. We are pleased to say that we have approved the plans to renovate the station as a museum. It will have links with the local City Museum and it will be operated by Aptrans – all year round. There'll be a gift shop and a Study Centre. This will

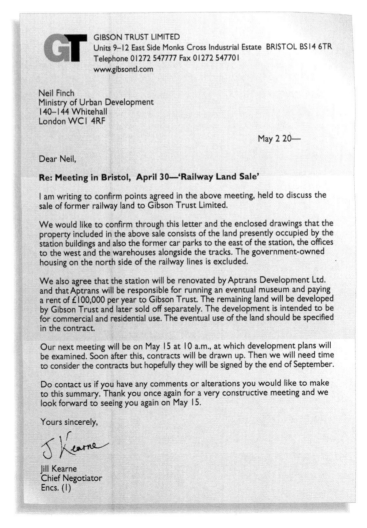

GIBSON TRUST LIMITED
Units 9–12 East Side Monks Cross Industrial Estate BRISTOL BS14 6TR
Telephone 01272 547777 Fax 01272 547701
www.gibsontl.com

Neil Finch
Ministry of Urban Development
140–144 Whitehall
London WC1 4RF

May 2 20—

Dear Neil,

Re: Meeting in Bristol, April 30—'Railway Land Sale'

I am writing to confirm points agreed in the above meeting, held to discuss the sale of former railway land to Gibson Trust Limited.

We would like to confirm through this letter and the enclosed drawings that the property included in the above sale consists of the land presently occupied by the station buildings and also the former car parks to the east of the station, the offices to the west and the warehouses alongside the tracks. The government-owned housing on the north side of the railway lines is excluded.

We also agree that the station will be renovated by Aptrans Development Ltd. and that Aptrans will be responsible for running an eventual museum and paying a rent of £100,000 per year to Gibson Trust. The remaining land will be developed by Gibson Trust and later sold off separately. The development is intended to be for commercial and residential use. The eventual use of the land should be specified in the contract.

Our next meeting will be on May 15 at 10 a.m., at which development plans will be examined. Soon after this, contracts will be drawn up. Then we will need time to consider the contracts but hopefully they will be signed by the end of September.

Do contact us if you have any comments or alterations you would like to make to this summary. Thank you once again for a very constructive meeting and we look forward to seeing you again on May 15.

Yours sincerely,

J Kearne

Jill Kearne
Chief Negotiator
Encs. (1)

be supported by the University and the City Library. Then we moved on to Item 2. We looked at plans for the other land, to be developed by Gibson Trust as – we agreed – 50% commercial property and 50% residential. This will be specified in the contract.

Finally, I'd like to confirm that what we have to do now is to finish drawing up contracts and then we'll meet again in late June. Probably on June the 25th, this has to be confirmed. At that meeting we will exchange contracts. Okay? Does everyone accept that as a reasonable summary?

PHOTOCOPIABLE © Cambridge University Press 2003

Timing: 15 minutes

Role play

The two role plays provide an opportunity to practise the target language of the unit.

- Allow 10–15 minutes' preparation and not more than 15 minutes to reach agreement.
- The negotiations should be quick and relatively simple.
- Students must reach an agreement and be able to summarise it at the end.
- They will need to take notes.
- A calculator might be useful.

Of the two situations offered, pairs of learners choose which they prefer.

1 Negotiating advertising space at football matches (File cards 15A and 15B).
2 Negotiating sale of a luxury flat in Tokyo's Shinjuku district (16A and 16B).

To ensure that all students practise both buying and selling, either have the class repeat the role play – if possible with different partners – or switch buying / selling roles and do the other situation.

Support the activity, give help where needed. Take notes.

At the end, get pairs to report on the deals reached. Ask students for their own comments and criticisms on what they have done. Ask them to say what went well and what was not successful. Provide similar comments yourself, then give language feedback.

Timing: 30 minutes (A generous estimation, including preparation and 15 minutes for each role play). If the option of doing both role plays is taken, allow more time.

Optional Case Study 1

Case Study 1 is a role play based on the situation introduced in Unit 13. Students should keep the same roles. You may choose to introduce this case study now, or leave it until after completing the final unit, Unit 15. If you choose to do it now, look at page 140.

Transfer

As usual, the Transfer task is designed to get students to reflect on their own experiences outside the classroom. Ask students to think about the questions asked for the next lesson. Then get them to volunteer any thoughts they had in response to the questions.

Skills Checklist

The Skills Checklist reiterates some of the key points about bargaining and making concessions. It also includes some new material on the role of different individuals in a negotiating team. Specifically, it refers to the roles of leading speaker and support speaker and contains some basic advice for each of these.

Check understanding of the items in the Checklist. Ask students which of the points made are particularly useful or relevant. Also, ask if they disagree with any of the recommendations.

Timing: 10 minutes

15 Not getting what you don't want

AIMS	■ Types of negotiator	■ Rejecting
	■ Dealing with conflict	■ Ending the negotiation

Briefing

This unit opens with a light-hearted look at negotiating style before examining the issue of conflict. Of course not all negotiations end in agreement, so the unit looks at unsuccessful as well as successful negotiations. The Skills Checklist includes reference to evaluating negotiations.

Language focus

The language focus is on dealing with conflict and rejection. There is opportunity for practice, including many short listening extracts as model answers to exercises. This prepares the way for the final role play, where the two teams have starting positions which are a long way apart, precipitating conflict and so testing students' ability to deal with difficulties. The likelihood is that this is one negotiation which will not result in agreement.

1:1 situation

There can be a lot of exploitation of taped material in this unit, which can be highly effective in 1:1 teaching. As usual, prompt the student as much as is necessary and take a role in the practice exercises and the role play. You can also alternate roles, where the students reads prompts in the Student's Book and you provide model answers.

Timing: 3.5 hours

1 Types of negotiator

This quick look at negotiating style echoes the section on Types of negotiation in Unit 13. Check recall of this before briefly discussing the negotiator

types which correspond to the three types of negotiation. Refer to the Skills Checklist in this unit.

The questionnaire should be completed in five minutes by students working in pairs. Go through the answers and elicit comments and discuss issues arising. Have students work out their score at the end to discover what kind of negotiator they are. Ask:

- Do students' scores in the questionnaire match how they actually see themselves as negotiators?
- Do different situations require different styles of negotiating? Elicit views on when different styles might be appropriate, or not.

Timing: 15 minutes

2 Dealing with conflict

Discuss the illustration. Ask students to suggest more appropriate language. Elicit a more moderate version, along the following lines: 'Can I explain our position? We think your prices are a little high, so we would like you to consider a lower price. Could you also confirm that the prices include delivery costs … Also, we've had some problems with previous orders, we'd like to hear any suggestions you may have about that … '

Ask what causes conflict in a negotiation. Brainstorm possible answers: incompatible / excessive demands, personality clashes, inappropriate attention to personal relationships, poor communication, lack of commitment, misunderstandings, cultural clashes, etc.

Option

Before students read the text, ask them how conflict can be reduced. More experienced and confident students might suggest the following:

- being aware of potential problems
- being well-prepared
- showing flexibility
- respecting the other side
- having a commitment to maintaining and developing the relationship.

1 Introduce the reading text. There are 13 ways to reduce conflict suggested in the text – all but the last bulleted point. The next question will help students understand more precisely several of these.

2 Check the matching with the key:

Key

- a) emphasise the benefits available to both sides
- b) invent new options for mutual gain
- c) change the package
- d) adjourn to think and reflect
- e) change location
- f) change negotiator (personal chemistry?)
- g) bring in a third party (mediator?)
- h) fix an off-the-record meeting

Check understanding of the other phrases, offering paraphrases for those too. Finally, deal with any outstanding vocabulary questions.

Timing: 15 minutes

3 Introduce the recording. Explain that students will hear several speakers in different negotiations using a variety of ways to resolve conflict. Make sure the task is clearly understood. Students have to match the recommendations in the box to the correct tape extract. Play each extract twice if necessary. Encourage listening for gist, not for every detail.

Key

a) (4)

b) (3)
c) (1)
d) (2)
e) (5)

Tapescript

Extract 1

I think we're not really making much progress. Perhaps it would be better to leave this point for a while and come back to it later. Could we talk about a different aspect to the deal, perhaps the question of delivery?

Extract 2

I think it is important to think about what could happen if we do *not* reach agreement. The most obvious consequence will be that we will both lose market share. The only winners will be our competitors. It could be serious for both of us.

Extract 3

There seem to be a number of problems, but I'd like to summarise the positive elements – issues where we have made progress. First, we agree that we have to settle the dispute between us, we understand how important this is. Second, we agree that the terms of our original agreement need to be changed. Third, we also agree that the change will depend on the different market conditions which affect our products … These are important points of progress.

Extract 4

Can I suggest we take a short break here? I think it will help if we look at some of the issues that are dividing us. Perhaps we will see areas where we can make a fresh offer.

Extract 5

The point at issue, Mr Cinis, is quite simple. We can offer you an extra 5% discount, but only if the order is increased by 20% over the next three years.

---

4 Students work in pairs to suggest suitable responses. Hear various suggestions before playing the recording. Check understanding, answer any questions.

Language focus option

Play the recording once more to focus on the examples given as models.

Pronunciation option

Throughout this unit, you may highlight aspects of pronunciation in the recorded extracts, notably stress of key words, intonation, pauses before key words, etc. Asking students to imitate what they hear is a good way to sensitise students to these important phonological features. The second recording with the model responses is especially suitable for particular examination of phonology.

Tapescript

Situation 1

A: The problem is that we have never offered the kind of warranty you are looking for.

B: Since we have a difficulty here, may I suggest we leave the problem of the warranty and come back to it later? Perhaps we could talk about training for our technical staff?

Situation 2

A: There's a number of issues on the table. We seem to be a long way from an agreement.

B: Can I suggest a lower price, but link this with us paying the shipment costs or agreeing to different payment terms?

Situation 3

A: The price you are asking is rather high, quite a lot higher than we were expecting.

B: Well, if it would help, we could agree to longer payment terms.

Situation 4

A: There are several problems. We think there is quite a lot of negotiation ahead before we can agree on a common strategy.

B: The benefits of reaching agreement are considerable. We will have more global influence and better prospects for the future.

PHOTOCOPIABLE © Cambridge University Press 2003

Timing: 45 minutes

Practice 1

Discuss the situation and clear up any uncertainties. Students can work in pairs or, in a large group, in fours, where two work together on one role, supporting each other, each contributing to the conversation.

Monitor students' efforts, suggest improvements. Then hear some examples performed for the whole class. If you think further practice is required, have individuals swap roles and choose a new partner to repeat the dialogue.

Finally, play the model version.

Timing: 20 minutes

Tapescript

SAR: Well, can we make you an offer? We would like to run the campaign for four extra weeks.

KPACK: Well, can we summarise the problem from our point of view? First of all, the campaign was late, it missed two important trade fairs. The ads also did not appear in two key magazines. As a result, it failed. Do you accept that summary of what happened?

SAR: Well, the delay was not entirely our fault. You did in fact make late changes to the specifications of the advertisements.

KPACK: Hmm … in fact, with respect, SAR were late with the initial proposals, so we had very little time, and in fact we only asked for small changes.

SAR: Well, whatever, can we repeat our offer to run the campaign for four extra weeks?

KPACK: That's not really the point. The campaign missed two key trade fairs – because of this we are asking you either to repeat the campaign next year, or we only pay 50% of the fee for this year.

SAR: Could we suggest a 20% reduction to the fee, together with a four weeks' extension to the campaign?

KPACK: We are not happy – the delays, the missed magazines, the trade fairs – we lost business.

SAR: I think we made mistakes, we both made mistakes. I think both sides are responsible.

KPACK: Okay, how about a new solution: how about a 40% cut in fee or a free repeat campaign?

SAR: But a full free campaign is impossible.

KPACK: I think we should have a break … we are not getting very far … perhaps we should have a think about this …

SAR: Perhaps, yes. We can talk about it.

3 Rejecting

Ask students to comment on the style of the rejection in the cartoon that opens the section. In fact, most rejections are much more delicate and tactful. Elicit some examples. Point out too that in many cases a frequent line is 'Thank you. We'll think about it' or 'We've got some other offers to consider'.

1 Introduce the situation. Check understanding, both of the situation and of the task. Play the recording and ask students to say which of the three responses is the most appropriate.

Key

A case could be made for both the second and third example. Discuss this with your students. In the second one, the speaker gives reasons for being unable to reach agreement and remains polite and calm, unlike the first speaker who seems very negative. The third is a common response, though probably a case of simply delaying saying no.

Tapescript

SPEAKER: In conclusion, we are prepared to provide you with a complete state-of-the-art photoprocessing laboratory. This equipment will give you an immediate technical advantage. The terms we offer you are very generous.
Response 1
Well, we've listened to the proposals you have made today and the plans you

have outlined. Basically, we have wasted time coming here.
Response 2
Well, we thank you for the efforts you have made, but we are very sorry. We do not feel able at this stage to accept your offer. Obviously, we have thought about it very carefully. The problem for us remains costs. We are not entirely convinced that the technical advantages justify the high cost. So, I think we are unable to reach agreement today. But, thank you for coming … we hope you'll contact us again with future offers.
Response 3
Well, if that is your final offer, thank you all for coming to see us. I think we are unable to give you a formal response today, but we will write to you and tell you of our decision in a day or two. Then we'll decide what the next step should be. So, thank you very much.

2 This exercise offers a rapid oral check on target language and can be done in class or as a self-study or homework task. Students can suggest any possible solutions, but if necessary, they can be helped by playing the Responses 2 and 3 from Exercise 3 again. There are other possible answers.

Key

a) Thank you for the efforts you have made, but *we are* very *sorry*.
b) We do not *feel able* at this stage to *accept* your offer.
c) Obviously, we have *thought about* it very carefully.
d) We are not entirely *convinced* that the technical advantages *justify* the high cost.
e) We hope you'll *contact* us again with future offers.
f) I think we are *unable* to give you a formal *response* today, but we will *write* to you and

tell you of our *decision* in a day or two.
Then we'll *decide* what the next step should
be. So, thank you very much.

3 This can also be done in class or as a self-study
or homework task.

Key

    a) Not at the moment.
    b) I'm afraid not.
    c) I doubt it.
    d) I'm afraid we just couldn't do that.

Practice 2

This exercise should be done in pairs without
preparation. Elicit efforts from various group
members. Eventually, play the model answers on
the recording and check understanding, deal with
any questions. Students can write the answers for
homework or self-study.

Pronunciation option

Use any of the recordings to focus specifically on
aspects of pronunciation. Ask students to identify
key words. Point out how the speaker stresses
words to convey his message and the falling
intonation of (affirmative) sentences.

Tapescript

Situation 1

A: Let me make a suggestion. If you agree to buy
100 units every month for the next twelve
months, we'll agree a 10% discount.

B: Unfortunately, I can't say how many we'll need
in six months and certainly not in 12. I can't
take the risk on such a large order at this stage.

Situation 2

A: The price we are offering excludes installation
costs but does include a 12 months' guarantee.

B: I'm afraid that's not really acceptable. You
know that other suppliers offer free installation
and a two-year parts and labour warranty?

Situation 3

A: I think the absolute minimum investment in
advertising must be $40,000, otherwise we
cannot reach enough of our market. It's not
much to ask for.

B: It's a pity, but it's still more than our budget. I
can't go that high.

Situation 4

A: Now, some excellent news: we'd like to increase
our order. Right now you are sending us 350
boxes a month. We need at least 500, demand
is very high …

B: Well, I'm glad you're having a lot of success with
our products, but the bad news is that our order
books are full, and the plant is working at full
capacity. We're a bit stuck, I'm afraid.

Practice 3

Clarify any questions about the flow chart, e.g.
margins – difference between costs and selling
price. Have students work in pairs, with minimal
preparation time. Hear some examples and elicit
feedback. Give additional advice.

For additional practice, students can switch
roles and / or change partners.

Tapescript

KROLL: Guten Tag. Kroll Auto.

ABACUS: Hello, this is Paul Bowen from Abacus in
the UK. I'd like to order some exhaust
pipes – 200 please, part number
DR5789032.

KROLL: No problem! When do you need them?

ABACUS: Immediately. Also, could we have a 10%
discount?

KROLL: Ah, you know our prices are already
discounted.

ABACUS: Er … can you tell me … what's the unit
price?

KROLL: One moment, I'll tell you … it's …
150 euros.

ABACUS: What about 135?

KROLL: I'd like to, but I'm sorry, our prices are
as low as we can make them. Just one
thing, we could do you a 2.5% discount
if payment is made at the time of order
– that is straightaway.

ABACUS: No, sorry. I can't do that. Could we agree
on a 5% discount with 60 days to pay?

KROLL: No, sorry, I can't agree to that. Margins
are very tight.

ABACUS: Yes, I know. It's always the same here too. Anyway, pity, but I'll call you again tomorrow, maybe you can do me a better offer.

KROLL: Good luck! Our prices are very competitive. But anyway, I look forward to your call. Bye for now!

ABACUS: Bye.

Timing: 45 minutes

4 Ending the negotiation

📼 ◎ **1** Have students work in pairs to decide if the words would indicate a positive or negative outcome of the negotiation. Play the recording to let students check their answers.

Key

(✗ = negative, ✓ = positive)

unfortunately ✗	another time ✗
no agreement ✗	not ready ✗
fruitful partnership ✓	problems ✗
very good ✓	satisfactory ✓
sorry ✗	useful ✓

Ask students to suggest other telltale words that might have been used (*very pleased / excellent / exciting potential* for positive outcome, *sadly / regret / haven't achieved* for negative outcome).

📼 ◎ **2** Play the recording again and have students complete the grid.

Key

Extract	Agreement reached?	Next step?
1	no	
2	yes	letter summarising agreement
3	yes	send specification in two weeks
4	no	
5	no	think – possibly renegotiate in a few days

Language focus option

Ask students to think about the sentiments expressed in the unsuccessful outcomes. Possibly the 'perhaps another time' and the 'perhaps in the future …' are not very genuine, but there seems to be some real regret and softening of positions in the last one.

Tapescript

Extract 1

I think it's clear we have *no agreement*. We're wasting time here, so thank you for talking to us, we've had a busy morning. I think we'll leave and perhaps *another time* we'll find some way to work together.

Extract 2

Well, I think that's been *useful*. I'll send you a letter summarising what we've agreed and look forward to a long and *fruitful partnership*.

Extract 3

If that's everything, I'd just like to say many thanks for coming today – it's been *very good*. I think we have a very *satisfactory* agreement and so, for the next step, we will send you the detailed specifications in two weeks.

Extract 4

So, I think we can both see that we are *not* quite *ready* to sign anything just now. Perhaps in future we may be able to reach agreement but, *unfortunately*, for the moment, we are some way apart. Anyway, thanks for coming, it's been interesting.

Extract 5

I'm *sorry* we've been unable to agree. It's a shame, but it looks like we need more time to settle our *problems*. In the meantime, I think we should have a think about the issues which are dividing us. Perhaps in the next few days our positions may change, in which case, we know how to contact each other.

Practice 4

Elicit suggestions orally. Offer them an example based on the first situation if necessary. At the end, play the recording of model versions.

Tapescript

Situation 1

It's been a long meeting, but finally I'm very glad we're able to reach agreement. I think it would be good if we could go on to a restaurant now, we'd be pleased if you can join us.

Situation 2

I'm sorry our efforts to reach agreement have not been successful. I suggest we stop here, but I hope that in the future we might work together on something.

Situation 3

Unfortunately, I feel it would be better if I don't join you on this project, but no doubt there'll be plenty of other things we'll work on.

Situation 4

I'd like to repeat our order, but not on those terms. I'm sorry, we can't agree to this. I think we'll go elsewhere, but thanks anyway.

Situation 5

I'm very sorry, but it really is physically impossible. We cannot supply goods in so short a time. It's just impossible. Sorry we can't help you.

Timing: 30 minutes

Role play

Divide the class into As and Bs. They should work in pairs, using the four situations on the cards. Remind them to use their own ideas as to how the negotiations should develop. They will see if they are successful or not. Remind them to use the target language heard in this unit. Refer to the Language Checklist.

With a large group, have students work in groups of four, two As and two Bs.

Each negotiation should last no more than five minutes.

As part of providing feedback, have one or two examples of the negotiations performed for the whole class, perhaps asking individuals who have not worked as pairs to spontaneously perform a negotiation based on one of the situations.

Use notes that you have made to provide a check on accurate use of target language.

Timing: 30 minutes

Transfers 1 and 2

Again, students may reflect on these questions for homework and bring their comments to the next lesson.

Skills Checklist

This is a detailed Skills Checklist with echoes of Unit 13 on types of negotiation. Here different types of negotiator are summarised. Elicit comments. Clarify as necessary. Ask students to identify the points they think are the most interesting or important.

Ask students if they think a negotiating team could usefully include one of each type of negotiator mentioned in the Checklist.

There are also ideas on evaluating negotiations. Students might like to discuss these and comment on how useful they are. As a practice exercise, they could evaluate the Role play negotiations at the end of the unit, or the Case studies.

Timing: 10 minutes

Optional case studies

Further practice is available through using the case studies which follow on page 121. Photocopy relevant material and hand out to the students.

The case studies will help to develop students' ability to use the language in this module, but also the language and skills studied throughout the course, especially Modules 3, 4 and 5.

Case study 1

This case study is an opportunity to employ a scoring method to assess the value of concessions made and gained. In this respect it can have a game-like atmosphere, instilling a degree of competitiveness into the negotiation while at the same time reminding students that negotiating concessions is concerned with loss and gain.

Ensure that the mechanics of the negotiation, as explained in the File cards, are clear to each team. Monitor their preparation and give help where required.

Note also that the case study is an opportunity to bring in skills examined in earlier units, especially presenting, chairing and participating in meetings. The extent to which the linking of different skills is achieved will depend on how much you promote the role play as an opportunity to revise the skills studied earlier in the course and how much time you make available for preparation and for the negotiation itself. Have students refer to previous modules and the Checklists in particular. Allow extra preparation time and encourage good teamwork, including the introduction of other issues not included in the File cards, if appropriate. Remind students that calling for an adjournment is a reasonable tactic if the meeting is not progressing

satisfactorily. Teams can then reassess their negotiating positions or strategies. *See notes on Feedback below.*

Case study 2

This case study is a Role play based on a new situation and designed to present a negotiation which may not reach a successful conclusion. It is also an opportunity for students to practise a range of skills developed during the course, including presentation skills, using visuals, meetings and negotiation skills. Exactly how much these are exploited depends on the time you make available to the use of the case study and the enthusiasm of the students for spending time on a fairly detailed approach to it.

The situation presented by File cards 19A and 19B could be dealt with relatively quickly – perhaps in less than half an hour. On the other hand, this is an opportunity for more detailed planning and a wide-ranging treatment involving several individuals. It is designed as a fairly fluid exercise. Monitor the preparation, encourage learners to add more details if they wish and to experiment with a fairly detailed negotiating position. Teams in particular should work out their position, decide roles and develop a coherent negotiating strategy.

In the course of preparing for the role play, encourage referring back to various relevant Skills and Language Checklists, including those of the final unit and dealing with conflict.

Feedback

As with other role plays in the course, encourage students to provide their own assessments of the good and the not so good aspects of the two role plays featured in these case studies. Elicit comments on how the negotiations went, the reasons for their success or otherwise, the good points and the areas that need improvement. Students should comment on their own performances as individuals, as teams and on the performance of the other side. The feedback can be entertaining and informative. It can also indicate where further work in required in terms of good communication skills and effective use of English.

Video-recording of the case study negotiations may be useful, not only for selective group feedback, but for teams and individuals to assess their work.

Case study 1

Here you have the opportunity to actually develop the negotiation which was introduced in Unit 13, concerning Coen Brothers and Fratelli Taviani.

- Work in groups A and B, *the same as you did in Unit 13* when preparing for the negotiation.
- Look again at your preparation for that negotiation.
- Follow the recommendations in Unit 14 on bargaining and making concessions. Try to use some of the language you heard and practised in that unit.
- Look at the Language and Skills Checklists in Unit 14.
- Look at the File cards:
  - Team A, Coen Brothers, turn to File card 17A.
  - Team B, Fratelli Taviani, turn to File card 17B.
- Plan roles within your team.

All the above will take you 20 minutes to prepare.

When you are ready, conduct the negotiation with the other party. If necessary, ask for adjournments so you and your team can reassess the progress and direction of the negotiation.

As an option at the end, prepare a short written report summarising the results.

Case study 2

This role play is designed to give further practice in bargaining and making concessions from Unit 14, as well as in dealing with conflict, rejecting and ending negotiations from Unit 15. However, you will also find that it is possible to use skills you have developed and language that you have studied in previous modules, especially Presentations and Meetings. It may be useful to refer back to the Language and Skills Checklists in those modules.

Situation

Your company is a subsidiary of HBT Inc., an American pharmaceuticals company. You are planning to set up a joint venture with colleagues from another subsidiary in a neighbouring country. You have to negotiate a plan for cooperation. You are both independent cost centres and the joint venture should (probably) be a 50–50 project.

Work in groups of between four and eight. These groups should divide into subgroups, A and B.

Teams A, from HBT Rexis Ltd., turn to File card 19A.

Teams B, from HBT Short Ltd., turn to File card 19B.

In preparing for the negotiation, remember to look again at the Language and Skills Checklists in Units 13 and 14.

5426058R00072

Printed in Great Britain
by Amazon.co.uk, Ltd.,
Marston Gate.